The West

Text by Giovanni Carrada

Illustrations by Sandro Rabatti

BARNES
&NOBLE
BOOKS
NEW YORK

DoGi

A Donati Giudici Associati Florence production

Originally published as *Il West*, 1995

This edition published by Barnes & Noble, Inc.,
by arrangement with DoGi spa

1998 Barnes & Noble Books

Text for original Italian edition by Giovanni Carrada

English translation by Elizabeth Leister

Illustrations by Sandro Rabatti, with contributions by Alessandro Bartolozzi,
Simone Boni, Giuliano Fornari, L.R. Galante, Paola Holguin, Loreno Orlandi,
Andrea Ricciardi, Claudia Saraceni, and Sergio

Picture research by Caroline Godard

Cover page and graphic design for original Italian-language edition by
Sebastiano Ranchetti

Text design for English language edition by Oxygen Design

ISBN 0-7607-0864-9

Printed and bound in Italy

98 99 00 01 02 03 M 9 8 7 6 5 4 3 2 1

DoGi

Table of Contents

THE GEOGRAPHY OF THE WEST

Endless seas of grass; rugged, towering mountains; forests of incredibly tall conifers; dramatic desert landscapes—these are just a few of the images that spring to mind when we think of the West. For centuries, "the West" meant new land to be explored and settled by European conquerors, immigrants, and their descendants. Likewise for centuries, what Americans called the West kept expanding and moving westward as explorers and settlers discovered the vastness of their new homeland. At the end of the eighteenth century, what is now Tennessee was thought of as the West. But when we speak of the West today, we generally mean the continental United States west of the Mississippi–the so-called "trans-Mississippi" West: from the grasslands of the prairies and the Great Plains, across the Rocky Mountains and the deserts of the Southwest, to the Pacific Coast.

The Rocky Mountains
These are the largest system of mountain ranges in North America. The Rockies extend from Canada to Mexico and are formed by some sixty mountain chains that run parallel to one another.

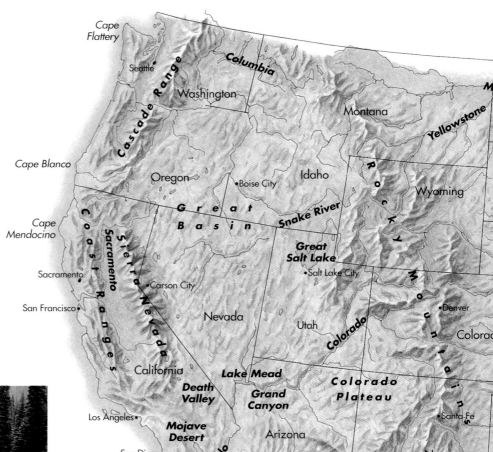

Forests
Enormous conifers grow in the chilly, humid Northwest. Dense forests of pines, cedars, and firs as much as 300 feet tall (over 90 m) form dense rain forests that cover the coastal region. The Rocky Mountains and the Sierra Nevada are other important forested areas.

The Great Basin
This is a vast arid depression in the intermontane region—the region between the Rockies and the Cascade Range and Sierra Nevada. The waters of the Great Basin have no outlet to the sea. With the exception of Utah's Great Salt Lake, the immense lakes that once existed in the Basin have all dried up.

The Sonoran Desert
This desert, which extends from southern Arizona and California to the states of Sonora and Baja California in Mexico, has the greatest abundance of animal and plant life of all North American deserts.

The Colorado River
The Colorado has its source in the Rocky Mountains and flows for 1,440 miles (2,320 km), passing through a desert plateau where the river and its tributaries have hollowed out deep canyons.

Sequoias

With a height of 395 feet (120 m) and a trunk diameter of about 30 feet (10 m), these are the biggest trees in the world. Sequoias, some of which are over 2,000 years old, grow only in California.

The Missouri River

Rising from three tributaries that have their source in the Rocky Mountains, the Missouri flows 2,314 miles (3,726 km) until it joins the Mississippi.

The Buffalo

At one time, enormous herds of buffalo roamed the North American prairies. Once almost completely killed off, it now survives in parks and reserves.

The Great Plains

An immense sea of grass, almost completely devoid of trees and furrowed by numerous rivers, the Great Plains stretch from Texas north into Canada and west to the Rocky Mountains.

The Mississippi River

The biggest river in North America, it has its source in Lake Itasca and flows for 2,346 miles (3,778 km), forming a very wide alluvial plain before it empties into the Gulf of Mexico.

The Grand Canyon

A spectacular gorge, about 280 miles (450 km) long and 1 mile (1,600 m) deep, it was carved by the waters of the Colorado River.

The Food Pyramid

All of the animals of the prairies depend, either directly or indirectly, on grass for their sustenance. The animals that make up the first link in the pyramid eat the grass. These animals are then a source of food for the predators, who in turn are hunted by the superpredators.

THE HISTORY OF THE WEST

The Spanish were the first Europeans to reach the West. At the end of the sixteenth century, they moved north from Mexico into California, where they later founded agricultural settlements and towns. The Americans did not begin to explore the West until after the Declaration of Independence in 1776. Around 1850, after a period of gradual exploration of the wild mountain regions by lone hunters, the real race to the West began. Americans and recently arrived European immigrants rushed westward in search of fertile land, pastures, and gold. Over the course of a few decades, the Native Americans, whom the Europeans called Indians, were forced onto small reservations, and their territories became new states in the American Union.

The First Humans
The history of the West is a history of settlement that began in very ancient times. The first humans arrived from Siberia thousands of years ago, and their descendants eventually formed the Indian tribes who occupied the vast lands west of the Mississippi when the Europeans first arrived in America around 1500.

Indian Territories in 1840

Peaceful Relations
In the beginning, the Europeans established peaceful relations with the Indians, acquiring land for settlements in exchange for alcohol, cloth, and weapons. The wars began when the settlers, driven by their need for land, began to violate the treaties with the Indians by taking their lands.

The Agricultural Boom
At the end of the nineteenth century, agricultural production in the United States increased enormously due to the introduction of efficient farm machinery. It was then that cereal crops replaced prairie land in the Great Plains.

Indian Territories in 1860

The Slaughter
Whole villages were destroyed. Many groups of people were deported to areas where they could find no way of supporting themselves. The massacre of the buffalo drove the Plains Indians to starvation. Those Indians not killed outright either died from diseases introduced by the whites or were corrupted by alcohol or weapons.

The Fur Trappers
Between 1820 and 1840, the wildest, most inaccessible areas of the Rocky Mountains were explored by fur trappers. Beavers, whose skins were very much in demand in the cities back East, were the favored game.

The Gold Rush
Between 1848 and 1852, tens of thousands of gold prospectors arrived in California, where they mined the gold deposits and built a great number of cities and mining towns. After they had extracted all the gold they could, they moved on to Colorado and Nevada.

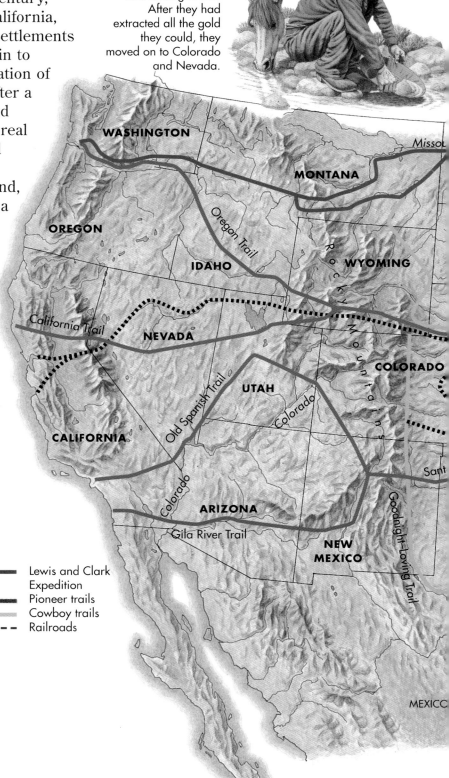

Lewis and Clark Expedition
Pioneer trails
Cowboy trails
--- Railroads

The Pioneers
Around 1850, tens of thousands of land-hungry settlers began to follow the trails heading west from the Mississippi. The pioneers traveled for months in slow wagon trains made up of dozens of wagons.

The First Explorations
Lewis and Clark were the first Americans to venture into the unexplored territories of the West. At the request of President Jefferson, their expedition set out from the Mississippi on 14 May 1804 and reached the Pacific coast in December of 1805.

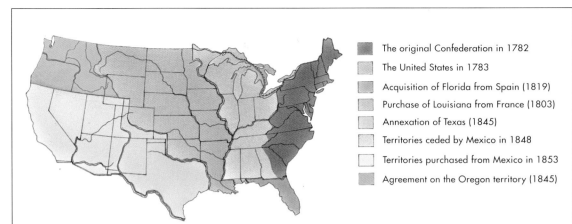

The original Confederation in 1782
The United States in 1783
Acquisition of Florida from Spain (1819)
Purchase of Louisiana from France (1803)
Annexation of Texas (1845)
Territories ceded by Mexico in 1848
Territories purchased from Mexico in 1853
Agreement on the Oregon territory (1845)

The Louisiana Purchase
In the early years of the nineteenth century, France resumed control of the vast Louisiana territory from Spain. But the reacquired territory no longer fit in with Napoleon's foreign policy goals, and in 1803, he decided to sell it. In just a few short weeks, his foreign minister, Talleyrand, and Jefferson's envoy, Robert R. Livingston, worked out an agreement on the price— $15 million. The transfer, dated 30 April 1803, opened the great vast spaces of the West to American settlement and doubled the size of the new nation.

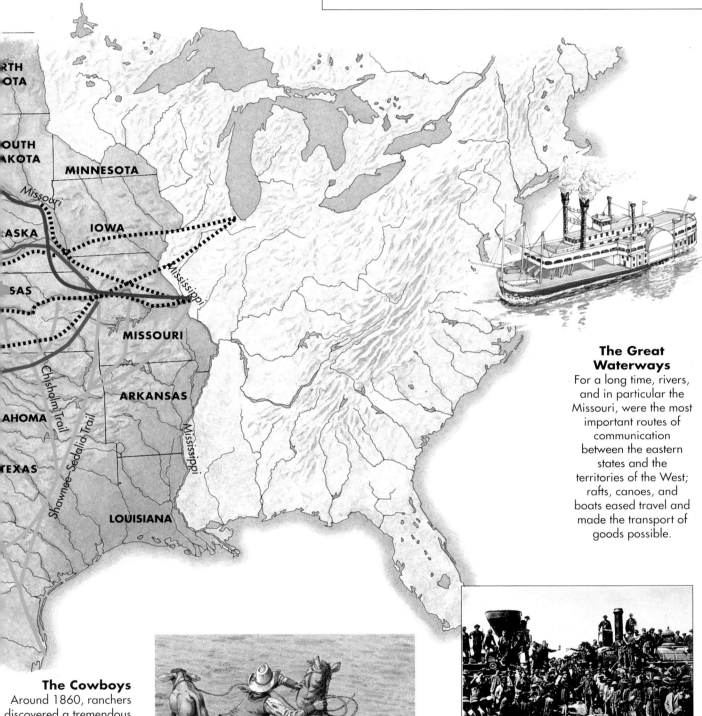

The Great Waterways
For a long time, rivers, and in particular the Missouri, were the most important routes of communication between the eastern states and the territories of the West; rafts, canoes, and boats eased travel and made the transport of goods possible.

Thomas Jefferson
Third president of the United States, Jefferson (1743–1826) sensed the enormous potential value of the territories west of the Mississippi; vast expanses where, up until the beginning of the nineteenth century, only brave hunters had ventured. He was convinced that it was these adventurous hunters who would open the way for the pioneers.

The Cowboys
Around 1860, ranchers discovered a tremendous source of profit in Texas: The cattle that had been left behind by the Spanish had reproduced in the wild, creating vast herds. So the ranchers hired cowboys to round up the cattle and move them from Texas to the cattle towns in the North.

The Railroad
The construction of the railroad linked the Mississippi Valley with the California coast once and for all. The work, entrusted to two competing companies (the Central Pacific and the Union Pacific) was finished in just five years (1864–69).

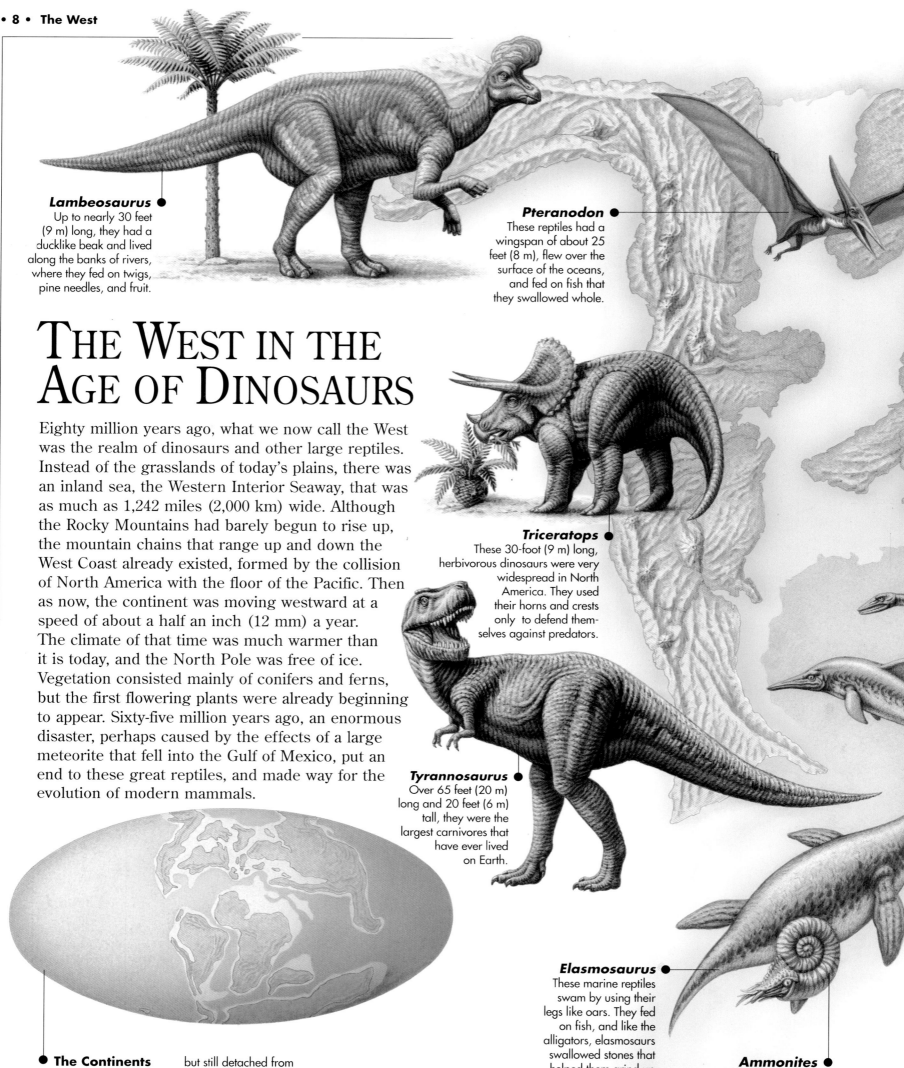

Lambeosaurus ●
Up to nearly 30 feet (9 m) long, they had a ducklike beak and lived along the banks of rivers, where they fed on twigs, pine needles, and fruit.

Pteranodon ●
These reptiles had a wingspan of about 25 feet (8 m), flew over the surface of the oceans, and fed on fish that they swallowed whole.

THE WEST IN THE AGE OF DINOSAURS

Eighty million years ago, what we now call the West was the realm of dinosaurs and other large reptiles. Instead of the grasslands of today's plains, there was an inland sea, the Western Interior Seaway, that was as much as 1,242 miles (2,000 km) wide. Although the Rocky Mountains had barely begun to rise up, the mountain chains that range up and down the West Coast already existed, formed by the collision of North America with the floor of the Pacific. Then as now, the continent was moving westward at a speed of about a half an inch (12 mm) a year. The climate of that time was much warmer than it is today, and the North Pole was free of ice. Vegetation consisted mainly of conifers and ferns, but the first flowering plants were already beginning to appear. Sixty-five million years ago, an enormous disaster, perhaps caused by the effects of a large meteorite that fell into the Gulf of Mexico, put an end to these great reptiles, and made way for the evolution of modern mammals.

Triceratops ●
These 30-foot (9 m) long, herbivorous dinosaurs were very widespread in North America. They used their horns and crests only to defend themselves against predators.

Tyrannosaurus ●
Over 65 feet (20 m) long and 20 feet (6 m) tall, they were the largest carnivores that have ever lived on Earth.

The Continents 80 Million Years Ago
At the time of the dinosaurs, North America was connected to Europe, but still detached from South America. The continents, in fact, are not stationary, but are slowly moving due to the pressure of the expanding ocean floor.

Elasmosaurus ●
These marine reptiles swam by using their legs like oars. They fed on fish, and like the alligators, elasmosaurs swallowed stones that helped them grind up food in their stomachs.

Ammonites ●
In the age of the dinosaurs, all of the world's seas were home to ammonites, predatory mollusks that are now extinct.

Styracosaurus
Over 16 feet (5 m) long, they were equipped with a horn similar to that of the rhinoceros and a crown of spikes used for defense.

Dromiceiomimus
The speed (31 mph or 50 kmh) of this small, no bigger than 10 feet (3 m) long, dinosaur allowed it to both escape from predators and to overtake and capture its own prey: insects, small mammals, and lizards.

Conifers
The West of 80 million years ago was covered with forests of conifers that were very similar to the sequoias, trees that still grow on the coastal ranges today.

Archelon
The shell of this sea turtle—over 12 feet (4 m) long—was formed by the bony ribs that grew out from its backbone. The ribs were covered with a thick, rubbery, leathery skin.

Camarasaurus
These herbivorous dinosaurs, which grew to as much as 60 feet (18 m) in length, had feet resembling those of the modern elephant.

Ichthyosaurus
About 6 feet (2 m) long, they resembled present-day dolphins, both in the shape of their bodies and because they also fed on small and medium-size fish.

Equus przewalskii

Pliohippus

Merychippus

Mesohippus

Hyracotherium

The Evolution of the Horse
About 20 million years ago, the ancestor of the horse first appeared in North America. This herbivorous mammal, the *Hyracotherium*, was about the size of a dog and had four toes on its front hooves and three on the back ones. Its descendants increased in size and lost all of the toes except for one, which we can still see on the wild horse, *Equus caballus przewalskii*. Before the end of the last ice age, about 15,000 years ago, the horse had disappeared in North America, but it continued to survive in Asia.

The horse died out in North America shortly before the arrival from Asia of another animal, man.

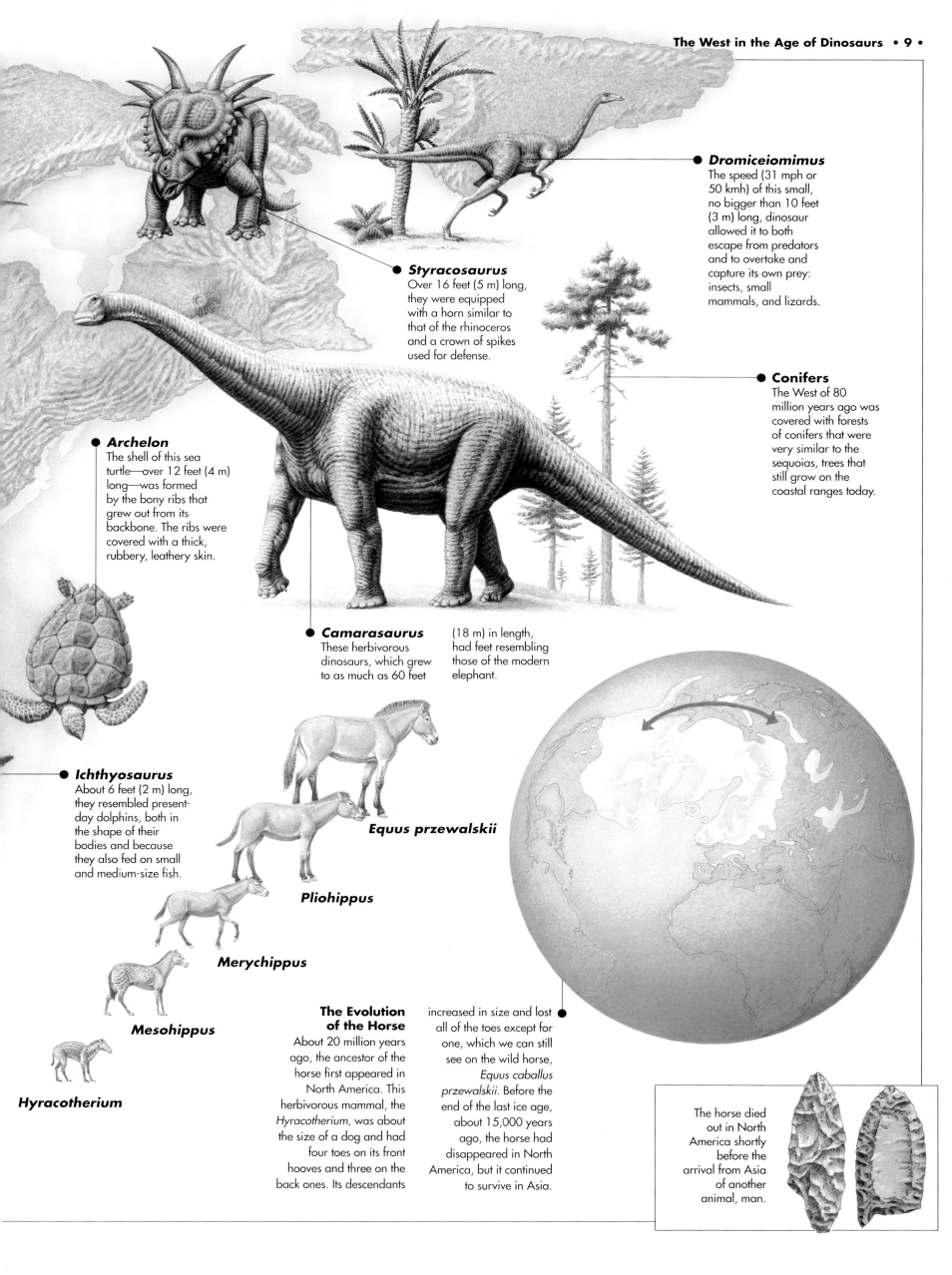

THE ARRIVAL OF MAN

When prehistoric man moved into North America, it was the beginning of the last great expansion of the human race toward the conquest of our planet. The small band of paleolithic hunters, perhaps scarcely a hundred in number, who first set foot on this immense, still virgin continent 11,500 years ago encountered animals that we can no longer see today: mammoths—huge land-dwelling sloths weighing up to three tons—beavers as big as bears, giant camels, saber-toothed tigers, and more. It was truly a hunter's paradise. But just a few centuries after the arrival of man, eighty species of these large mammals had already disappeared. According to some scholars, it was these first hunters who caused the animals to die out. But could the primitive weapons of prehistoric man really have destroyed so many animals? Perhaps it is possible, since these creatures had never seen human beings and so were not afraid of them.

The First American?
This jaw of a baby is one of the oldest human remains found in North America and is at least 27,000 years old. It was found in Old Crow, in the Yukon, in 1966 by Peter Lord, an Indian hunter from the Loucheaux tribe.

● **23,000–10,000 B.C.**
The oldest, still rather rudimentary, spear-heads were used for hunting mammoths, animals that at that time lived in the area that straddled Siberia and Alaska, most of which is now under water.

Titanotylopus
Over 11 feet (3.5 m) tall at the shoulder, it was apparently very similar to the modern camel, but the characteristic accumulations of fat on the back were much smaller.

Platygonus
A mammal of both the forests and the open plains, it was about 3 feet (1 m) in length. It lived on the tubers and roots that it found with its nose, which was similar to a pig's snout. Its long sharp canines were used for defense.

Settlement
Bands of Siberian hunters reached Alaska about 27,000 years ago at the height of the last ice age, when the Bering Strait could be crossed on foot. Then about 11,500 years ago, an ice-free corridor to the south opened up. Settlement was very rapid: In just seven centuries, the descendants of those first hunters reached the southern tip of South America.

Smilodon
This saber-toothed tiger, a little more than 3 feet (1 m) in length, was one of the most powerful predators in the ancient West. Its great fangs were even able to pierce the hide of the largest of its prey, like the buffalo and the mammoth.

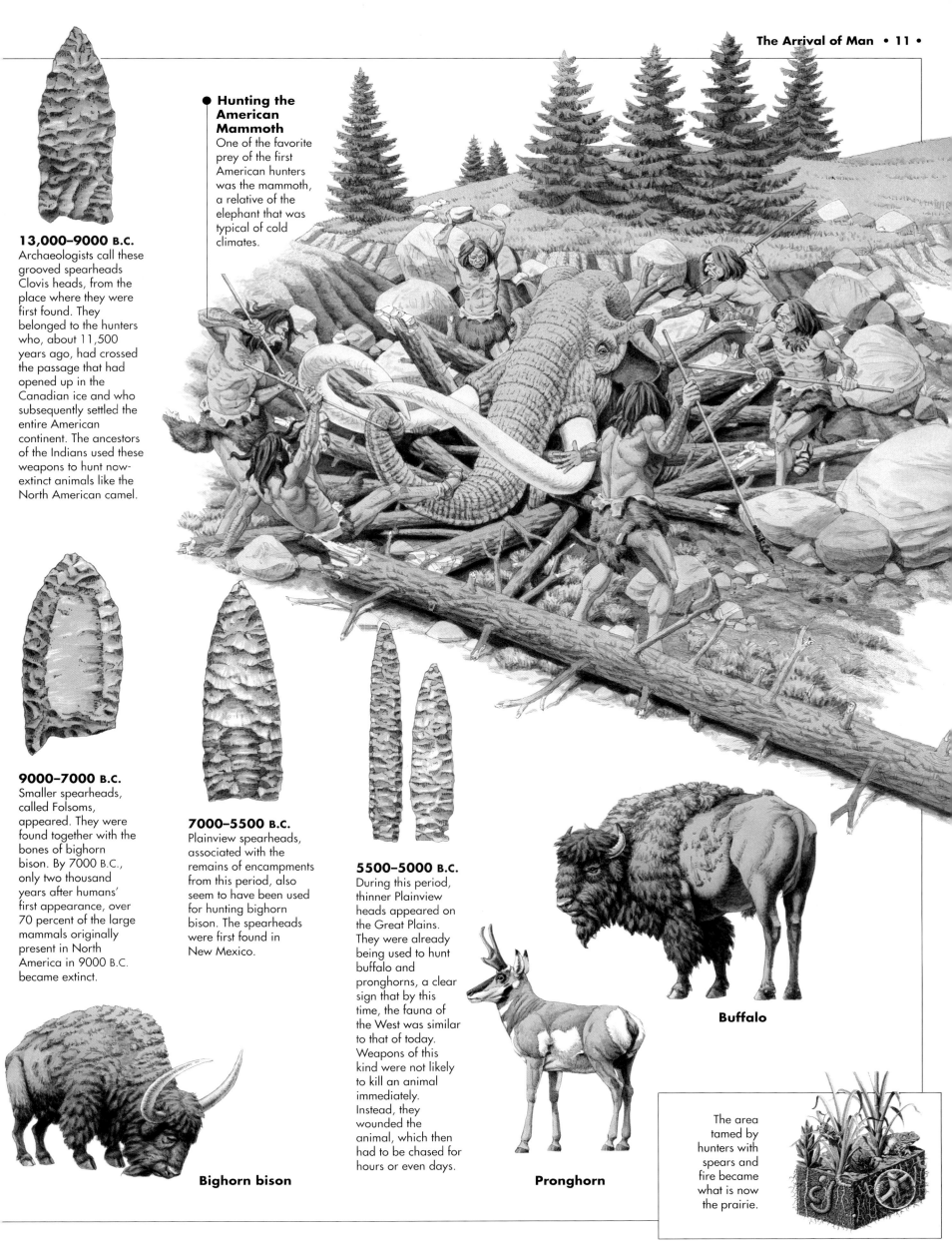

13,000–9000 B.C.
Archaeologists call these grooved spearheads Clovis heads, from the place where they were first found. They belonged to the hunters who, about 11,500 years ago, had crossed the passage that had opened up in the Canadian ice and who subsequently settled the entire American continent. The ancestors of the Indians used these weapons to hunt now-extinct animals like the North American camel.

● **Hunting the American Mammoth**
One of the favorite prey of the first American hunters was the mammoth, a relative of the elephant that was typical of cold climates.

9000–7000 B.C.
Smaller spearheads, called Folsoms, appeared. They were found together with the bones of bighorn bison. By 7000 B.C., only two thousand years after humans' first appearance, over 70 percent of the large mammals originally present in North America in 9000 B.C. became extinct.

7000–5500 B.C.
Plainview spearheads, associated with the remains of encampments from this period, also seem to have been used for hunting bighorn bison. The spearheads were first found in New Mexico.

5500–5000 B.C.
During this period, thinner Plainview heads appeared on the Great Plains. They were already being used to hunt buffalo and pronghorns, a clear sign that by this time, the fauna of the West was similar to that of today. Weapons of this kind were not likely to kill an animal immediately. Instead, they wounded the animal, which then had to be chased for hours or even days.

Buffalo

Bighorn bison

Pronghorn

The area tamed by hunters with spears and fire became what is now the prairie.

Location of the three bands of the Great Plains

The western band of the Great Plains is the most arid and has short, sparse grass.

The central band, with medium rainfall, has grass of medium height.

The wettest, eastern band has tall, thick grass.

THE PRAIRIE ECOSYSTEM

The prairie is a very rich ecosystem capable of feeding many different kinds of animals. But above all, it is a realm of herbivores, grass-eating animals that almost always range the prairie in groups. The reason for this is simple: The prairie is an immense open space that offers little or no natural cover, and at least one of the animals must always be on guard for dangerous predators in order to warn the group. Some creatures, like the striped ground squirrel, take shelter in deep burrows at the least sign of danger, while others, like the pronghorn, run till out of danger. Then there is the little gopher that only leaves his den after sundown. But the prairie is not only a fruitful environment; it is also a harsh one, very hot in the summer and extremely cold in the winter. As a result, many animals, like the buffalo, migrate seasonally in order to find better conditions, while others, like the prairie dog, go into hibernation in the winter.

The Soil
Many small animals live in the prairie soil. Nematodes, earthworms, and other invertebrates incessantly rework the soil, aerating the roots of plants, and recycling the organic matter produced by these plants. Their actions, combined with those of microorganisms, enrich the soil with mineral nutrients. In addition, these small animals are the favorite food of a great number of birds and mammals.

The Buffalo
Nearly 7 feet (2 m) in height and 10 feet (3 m) in length, the buffalo is the largest mammal in the Americas. Before the arrival of Europeans, the great buffalo herds numbered about 70 million head.

The Coyote
A carnivore similar to the wolf but smaller in size, the coyote lives alone or in pairs, and eats hares, small rodents, large insects, and carrion. It is even able to catch prairie dogs and pronghorns.

The Wolf
It is a large carnivore, over 6 feet (2 m) in length, that hunts in packs. Its favorite prey include pronghorns, prairie dogs, and, with a bit of luck, small buffaloes.

The Sage Grouse
A very shy bird, it feeds on leaves and twigs.

The American Badger
This carnivore, with its long shaggy coat, can be readily identified by the white stripe on its head. It feeds on rodents, small reptiles, birds, and insects, and in turn, it is the prey of coyotes and eagles.

The Prairie Falcon
About 16 inches (40 cm) long, this winged predator lives on the prairies and high plains of North America.

The American Kestrel
About 8 inches (20 cm) long, this raptor mainly hunts insects in the summer, while in the winter it preys on small birds and rodents.

The Red-tailed Hawk
Easily identified by the color of its tail, this bird of prey grows to 25 inches (65 cm) in length and feeds on rodents and other small vertebrates.

The Golden Eagle
With a wingspan of almost 7 feet (2 m), this is the largest bird of prey that can be seen flying over the prairies during the daytime as it searches for prey.

The Burrowing Owl
Widespread in almost all of America, it lives in tunnels dug by prairie dogs and other mammals, or it digs its own. It catches small reptiles and mammals, insects, and amphibians either by flying close to the ground or by running them down.

Superpredators

Predators

Herbivores

The Food Pyramid
1. Red-tailed hawk;
2. wolf; 3. golden eagle;
4. great horned owl;
5. polecat; 6. praying mantis; 7. coyote;
8. American badger;
9. royal falcon;
10. long-tailed weasel;
11. burrowing owl;
12. prairie falcon;
13. diamondback rattlesnake;
14. jackrabbit;
15. buffalo; 16. thirteen-striped ground squirrel;
17. grasshopper;
18. calandra sparrow;
19. Virginia quail;
20. greater prairie chicken; 21. prairie dog; 22. pronghorn;
23. mule deer; 24. plains gopher.

The Pronghorn
This herbivore, about 5 feet (1.5 m) in length, has very special horns: They are hollow, like those of cattle, but are also shed, like those of deer. Its speed (40 mph or 65 kmh) allows it to escape predators. Once 40 million pronghorns lived on the prairies, but today only 500,000 of them survive.

The Black-footed Ferret
Only about a hundred specimens of this small carnivore survive in all of North America.

The Green Rattlesnake
A poisonous snake about 3 feet (1 m) long, it is very common on the prairies. It frightens aggressors by shaking the end of its tail, making a sharp rattling sound.

The Prairie Dog
This rodent, about 12 inches (30 cm) in length, digs burrows that also provide shelter for many other animals.

Before the arrival of Europeans, Native Americans also fit into this ecosystem in a natural way.

THE WEST BEFORE EUROPEANS

Many of the native peoples of North America led a largely nomadic life. Over the course of centuries, they moved among the plains, the mountains, the deserts, and the coastline. Therefore, where the various tribes lived and the overall population distribution in the West were never constant. And the tribes not only lived in very different places, but also came up with very different systems for survival. Along the coast of California, and as far north as Alaska, were tribes who mainly lived off salmon fishing and gathering seaweed. In California and elsewhere the Native Americans were hunters, taking advantage of the plentiful game. In the arid areas of the Southwest, the Pueblo tribes—so-called by the Spanish because they lived in villages, that is, "pueblos," made of stone or adobe—lived off agriculture. But the most difficult environment for humans trying to eke out a living in the West was the desert. The tribes who lived there survived by hunting, and especially, by gathering roots. And finally, the peoples of the plains hunted buffalo in the great grassy expanses west of the Mississippi.

The Wallawalla
They lived along the Columbia River, and like other Native Americans of the Northwest, they were salmon fishers. Each year, millions of these fish swam upstream from the ocean to spawn.

The Navajo
Originally from northwestern Canada and Alaska, by 1492 they had arrived in the Southwest. While the Navajos preserved their native language, quite different from that of neighboring tribes, they learned how to become expert farmers from these tribes.

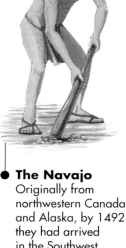

The Chumash
The Chumash made their home on the coast of southern California near present-day Santa Barbara, and lived by hunting and fishing. Skillful builders of canoes and good navigators, they settled the islands off the coast.

The Hopi
Even today, they still live in their typical adobe brick and stone villages, the pueblos, and one of their chief occupations is growing corn. This grain personifies their most important god, to whom they pray for rain for their crops.

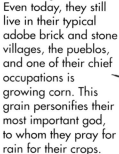

The Paiutes
They were a nomadic tribe who moved along fixed routes throughout the year. They were hunters and gatherers like other peoples of the Great Basin, but unlike similar tribes, the Paiutes had learned how to build small dams and systems of canals to irrigate the soil for the wild plants that they lived on.

The Pomo
Like other tribes on the California coast, they essentially lived off fishing and hunting. During the hunt, the men covered their heads with the head of a deer in order to attract fresh prey. The women were in charge of gathering the acorns that were then ground up for flour.

SALISH WALLAWALLA
WASHINGTON
MONTAN
OREGON
SHOSHONE
IDAHO
POMO
PAIUTE
NEVADA
WYO
UTE
CHUMASH
UTAH
CALIFORNIA
N
ME
ARIZONA
HOPI

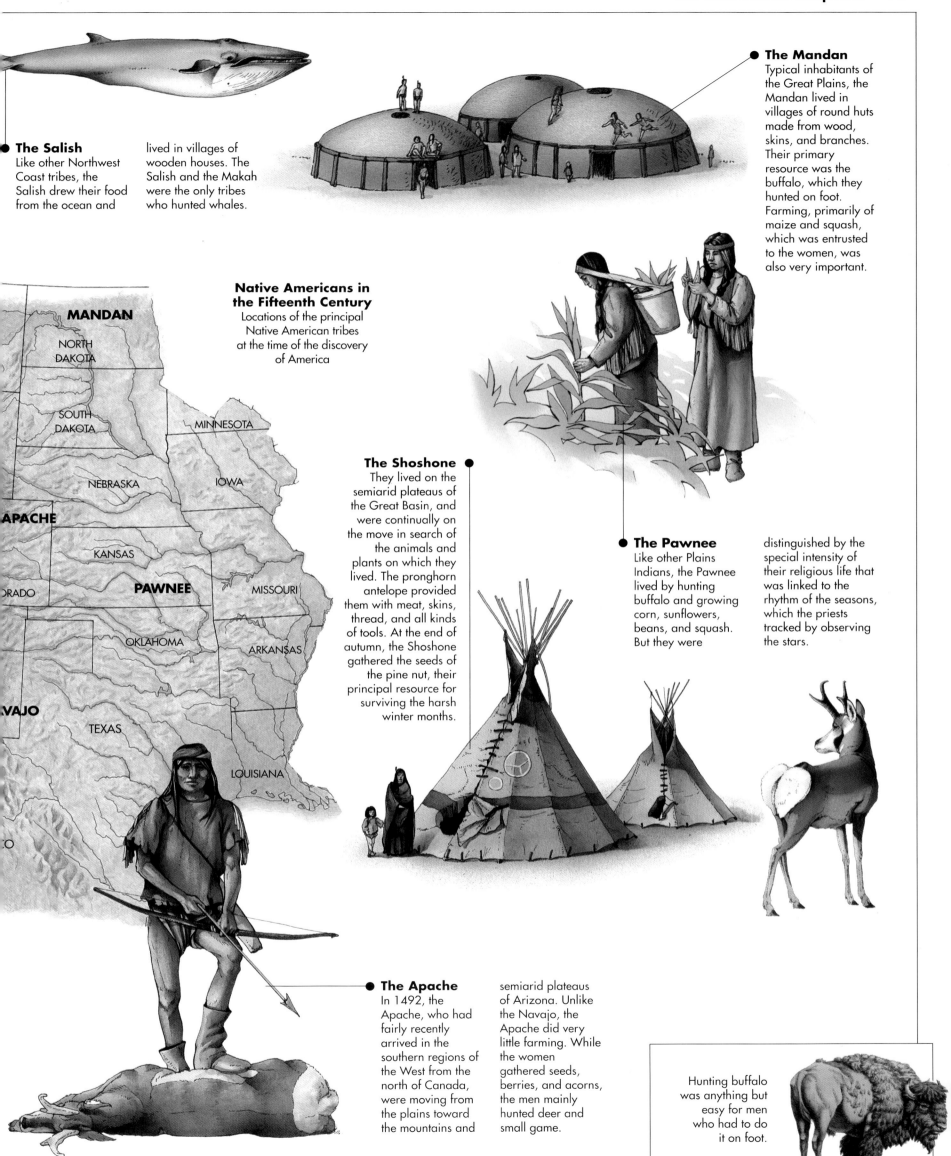

The Salish
Like other Northwest Coast tribes, the Salish drew their food from the ocean and lived in villages of wooden houses. The Salish and the Makah were the only tribes who hunted whales.

The Mandan
Typical inhabitants of the Great Plains, the Mandan lived in villages of round huts made from wood, skins, and branches. Their primary resource was the buffalo, which they hunted on foot. Farming, primarily of maize and squash, which was entrusted to the women, was also very important.

Native Americans in the Fifteenth Century
Locations of the principal Native American tribes at the time of the discovery of America

MANDAN

NORTH DAKOTA

SOUTH DAKOTA

MINNESOTA

NEBRASKA

IOWA

APACHE

KANSAS

PAWNEE

MISSOURI

ORADO

OKLAHOMA

ARKANSAS

VAJO

TEXAS

LOUISIANA

O

The Shoshone
They lived on the semiarid plateaus of the Great Basin, and were continually on the move in search of the animals and plants on which they lived. The pronghorn antelope provided them with meat, skins, thread, and all kinds of tools. At the end of autumn, the Shoshone gathered the seeds of the pine nut, their principal resource for surviving the harsh winter months.

The Pawnee
Like other Plains Indians, the Pawnee lived by hunting buffalo and growing corn, sunflowers, beans, and squash. But they were distinguished by the special intensity of their religious life that was linked to the rhythm of the seasons, which the priests tracked by observing the stars.

The Apache
In 1492, the Apache, who had fairly recently arrived in the southern regions of the West from the north of Canada, were moving from the plains toward the mountains and semiarid plateaus of Arizona. Unlike the Navajo, the Apache did very little farming. While the women gathered seeds, berries, and acorns, the men mainly hunted deer and small game.

Hunting buffalo was anything but easy for men who had to do it on foot.

THE PLAINS INDIANS

When Europeans first arrived in North America, the most typical inhabitants of the Great Plains were the Mandan. Their ancestors had come to the northern plains from Mexico, where they had learned how to grow corn. They also learned the secrets of growing sunflowers from neighboring Plains tribes. But one of their major resources was the buffalo. Immense herds of these animals migrated from north to south and south to north, season after season, in search of the best pasturelands. Before the arrival of the horse, the buffalo hunt was carried out on foot, but facing the buffalo in the open was unthinkable! So every year, Mandan hunters hid near a natural precipice, generally close to a river, and awaited the passage of the migrating herds. With fire and loud noises, groups of hunters tried to frighten the animals and force them to head toward the precipice at full speed. By the time the buffalo realized that they were caught in a trap, it was already too late. If the hunters' strategy was successful, they would then be able to slaughter the fallen animals. The hunt was not only very difficult, but extremely dangerous, because the buffalo could also charge the hidden hunters and trample them.

The Okipa Ceremony
This took place every year in the middle of the summer and lasted for several days. The young males withstood a series of tortures in which they had to prove that they had the necessary strength and courage for war and for the buffalo hunt. In the most painful ordeal, they were hung from the ceiling of the ceremonial lodge with wooden hooks driven into their arms, chest, and legs.

Their Territories
The Mandan lived in the northern plains in what is now North Dakota.

Fire
Large fires were set on the prairies to burn off the old grass and speed up new growth and thus attract the buffalo to the hunting grounds the following year.

The Slaughter
The buffalo that had been wounded in the fall were killed and then butchered with simple stone knives. Every part of the animal was used.

Cooperation
Using signals, a few hunters stationed on high ground showed their companions which way to drive the herd of buffalo.

Their Lodges
The round lodges of Mandan villages were covered with earth resting on a framework of willow trunks. These houses provided effective shelter from the wind, the cold of winter, and the heat of summer.

The High Ground
This was an ideal observation post to await the arrival of the herds.

Farther to the south, other Indians had built large villages entirely of masonry, the biggest construction projects in North America.

Farmers
The Anasazi were an agricultural people whose principal crops were corn and beans. These protein-rich legumes were a very important part of their diet because these Indians did not raise domestic animals.

THE ANASAZI

Between the years 900 and 1100, the Indians of the Four Corners Region, the Anasazi, began to erect the largest masonry structures in ancient North America, the pueblos. The biggest of these was Pueblo Bonito in Chaco Canyon—five stories high, and 722 feet (220 m) long, 334 feet (105 m) wide, with 250 rooms. Today, its ruins rise in a completely uninhabited, semidesert area. Why on earth did the Anasazi build this great pueblo in such an inhospitable place? Archaeologists have discovered that at the time it was built, Chaco Canyon was surrounded by large forests of pines and junipers, and abundant springs supplied the Anasazi's houses and fields with water. The Anasazi began to cut down the trees to use for both building and heating.

Their Territories
The Anasazi lived in the area where Arizona, New Mexico, Utah, and Colorado come together.

But over time they had to go farther and farther afield to find the trees they needed, because in the climate of the Southwest, the trees did not grow back fast enough. Once the trees that had retained the moisture from the rains had disappeared, the springs also dried up. Longer and longer roads and aqueducts had to be built to supply Chaco Canyon, until not even these efforts were enough anymore, and the pueblo had to be abandoned. And so the entire Anasazi civilization disappeared as the result of a serious ecological stress.

The Sword of the Sun
This sundial was built at the entrance to Chaco Canyon. The shadows cast by the three vertical stones indicated the equinoxes and solstices on the bas-relief. These dates were important for the farmers, who had to schedule their work according to the growing seasons.

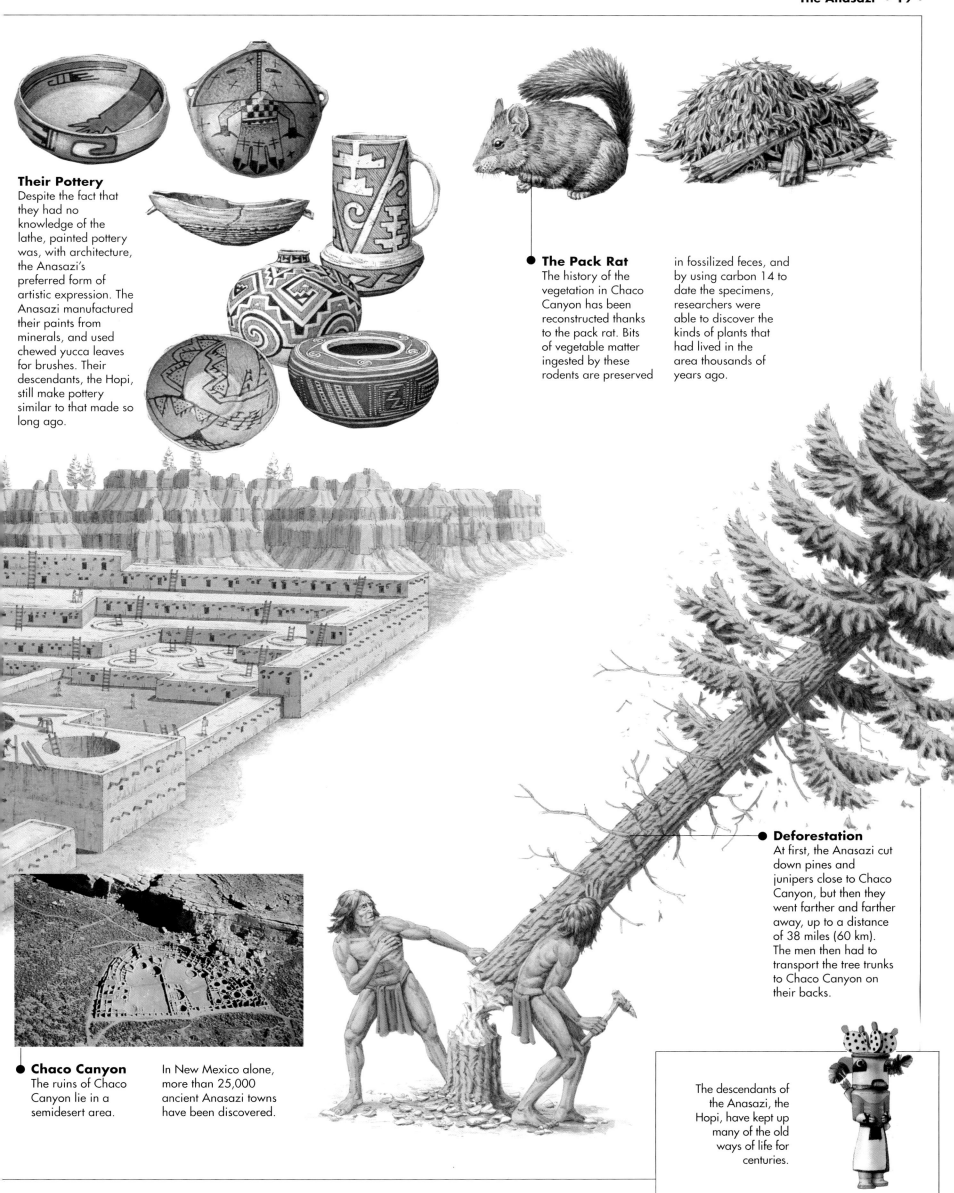

Their Pottery

Despite the fact that they had no knowledge of the lathe, painted pottery was, with architecture, the Anasazi's preferred form of artistic expression. The Anasazi manufactured their paints from minerals, and used chewed yucca leaves for brushes. Their descendants, the Hopi, still make pottery similar to that made so long ago.

The Pack Rat

The history of the vegetation in Chaco Canyon has been reconstructed thanks to the pack rat. Bits of vegetable matter ingested by these rodents are preserved in fossilized feces, and by using carbon 14 to date the specimens, researchers were able to discover the kinds of plants that had lived in the area thousands of years ago.

Deforestation

At first, the Anasazi cut down pines and junipers close to Chaco Canyon, but then they went farther and farther away, up to a distance of 38 miles (60 km). The men then had to transport the tree trunks to Chaco Canyon on their backs.

Chaco Canyon

The ruins of Chaco Canyon lie in a semidesert area.

In New Mexico alone, more than 25,000 ancient Anasazi towns have been discovered.

The descendants of the Anasazi, the Hopi, have kept up many of the old ways of life for centuries.

THE HOPI

The Hopi, whose name means "peaceful people," have lived on the arid soil of Arizona and New Mexico since the beginning of the twelfth century. The survival of their culture in such an inhospitable place testifies to their perfect understanding of the natural environment. Hopi traditions have remained unchanged almost until the present day. The Hopi still live in villages built on the mesas, high plateaus or tablelands with steep sides. In Hopi society, it is the women who own the houses, food, seeds, springs, and fields, while the men hunt, work the fields, and attend to religious life. For centuries, Hopi religious practices have revolved around the seasonal movement of the Sun, on which they base the scheduling of work in the fields and the growing of maize, or Indian corn. This plant embodies the Hopi's most important divinity: Mother Maize, to whom they pray for rain.

Their Territories
The Hopi lived in the area once occupied by the Anasazi.

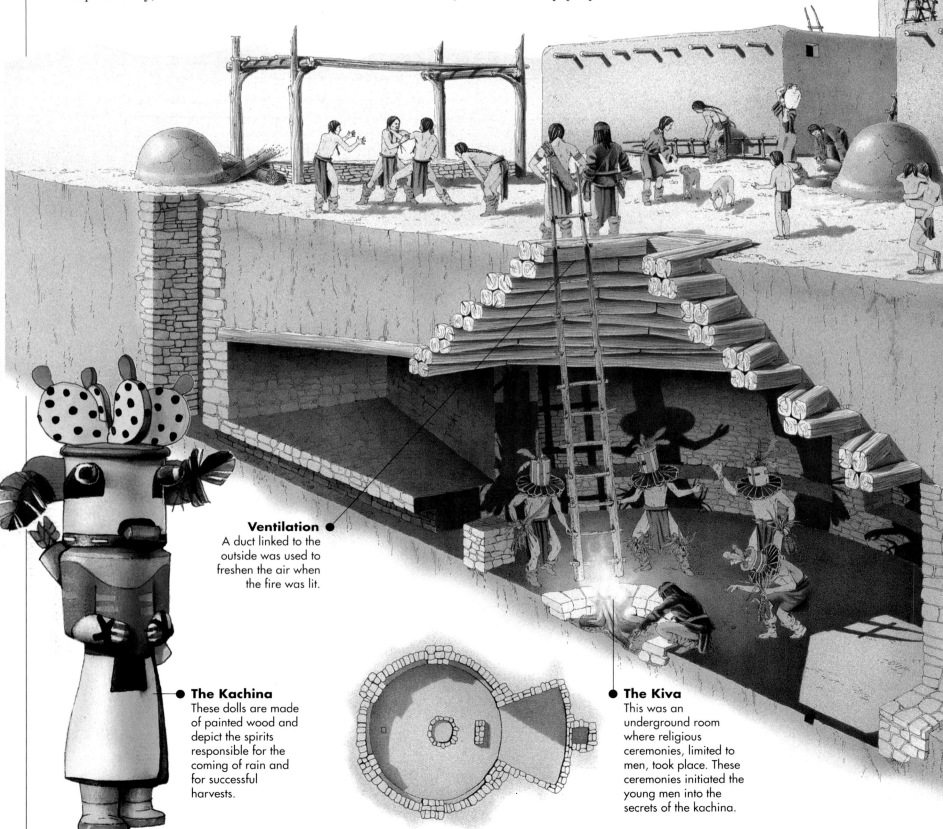

Ventilation
A duct linked to the outside was used to freshen the air when the fire was lit.

The Kachina
These dolls are made of painted wood and depict the spirits responsible for the coming of rain and for successful harvests.

The Kiva
This was an underground room where religious ceremonies, limited to men, took place. These ceremonies initiated the young men into the secrets of the kachina.

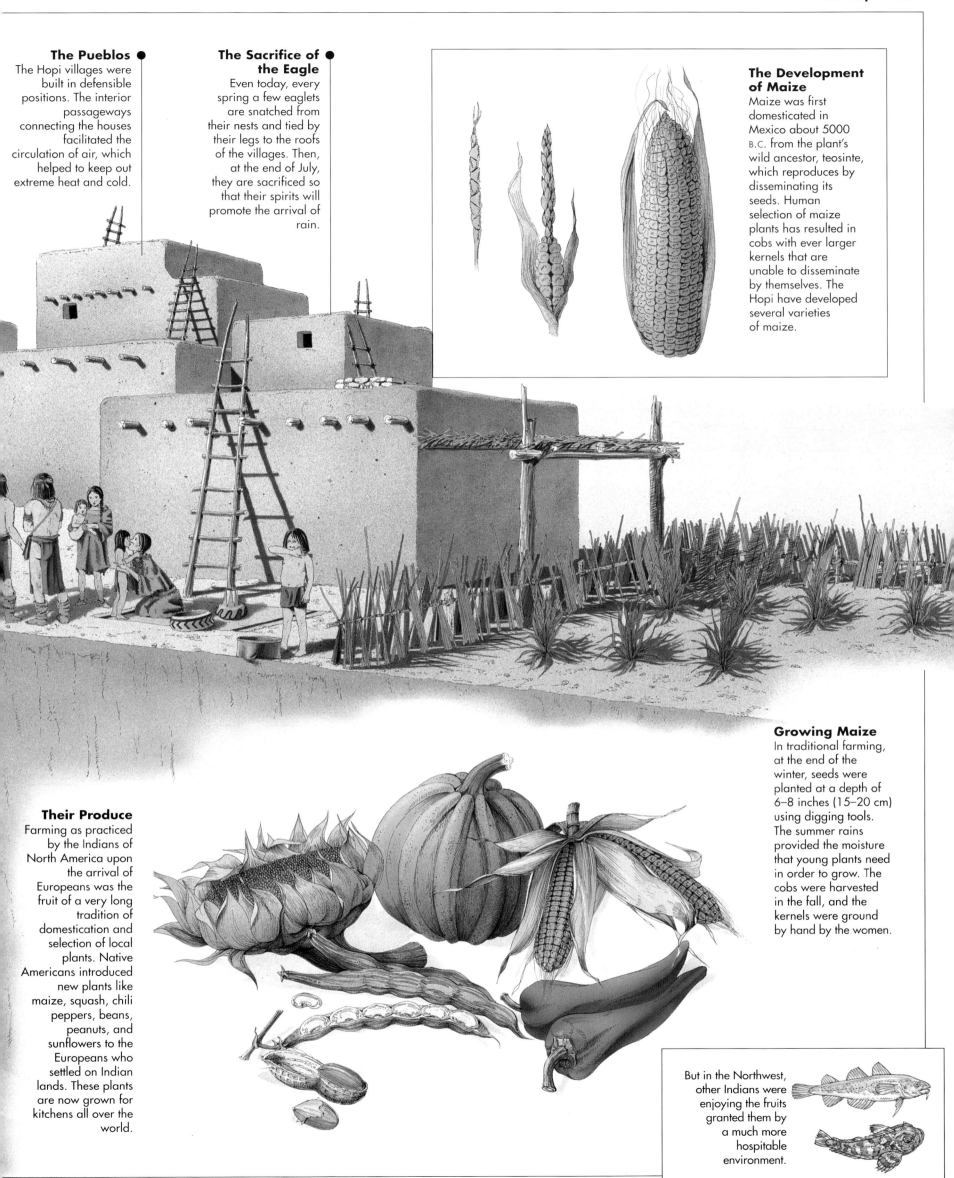

The Pueblos
The Hopi villages were built in defensible positions. The interior passageways connecting the houses facilitated the circulation of air, which helped to keep out extreme heat and cold.

The Sacrifice of the Eagle
Even today, every spring a few eaglets are snatched from their nests and tied by their legs to the roofs of the villages. Then, at the end of July, they are sacrificed so that their spirits will promote the arrival of rain.

The Development of Maize
Maize was first domesticated in Mexico about 5000 B.C. from the plant's wild ancestor, teosinte, which reproduces by disseminating its seeds. Human selection of maize plants has resulted in cobs with ever larger kernels that are unable to disseminate by themselves. The Hopi have developed several varieties of maize.

Growing Maize
In traditional farming, at the end of the winter, seeds were planted at a depth of 6–8 inches (15–20 cm) using digging tools. The summer rains provided the moisture that young plants need in order to grow. The cobs were harvested in the fall, and the kernels were ground by hand by the women.

Their Produce
Farming as practiced by the Indians of North America upon the arrival of Europeans was the fruit of a very long tradition of domestication and selection of local plants. Native Americans introduced new plants like maize, squash, chili peppers, beans, peanuts, and sunflowers to the Europeans who settled on Indian lands. These plants are now grown for kitchens all over the world.

But in the Northwest, other Indians were enjoying the fruits granted them by a much more hospitable environment.

OZETTE, THE POMPEII OF THE NORTHWEST

About five hundred years ago, in a matter of a few minutes, a mud slide buried Ozette, the largest of the five Makah villages of the time. Although this disaster destroyed the village, it also preserved the secrets of Makah life. Like other Indians in the Northwest, the Makah were extraordinarily favored by nature. In spring and summer, millions of salmon swam up the rivers of this coastal region. The area was blessed with abundant rainfall, and as a result, there were dense conifer forests in the mountains that provided the Makah with timber and wild berries. But the Makah's primary resource was the ocean, rich in mollusks, fish, seals, and whales. They ventured onto the sea in canoes dug out of cedar trunks. Even though the Makah did not know how to extract iron, they did have small metal axes and knives retrieved from the wreckage of Chinese junks that had been washed up on their shores by the ocean currents.

The Discovery
In 1970, the ruins of Ozette were brought to light by a violent storm. Objects made of wood—the basic material of Makah technology—and large quantities of animal bones had been preserved for centuries. These artifacts enabled archaeologists to reconstruct the life of these ancient Indians.

Location
Ozette stood at the tip of Cape Alava in what is now Washington State, an ideal location for hunting seals and whales.

A Favorable Climate
Despite its latitude, even in the winter this area enjoys moderate temperatures because the current from Japan carries warm, rain-laden air to the coast.

Their Houses

Their houses, each one home to several families, were about 95 feet (30 m) long and 35 feet (10 m) wide, and built of cedar boards. The joints between the boards were filled with seaweed and mosses. A series of benches were lined up along the inside walls and served as simple beds at night.

The Wood
The Makah used red alder for containers, and yew for bows, paddles, and hooks.

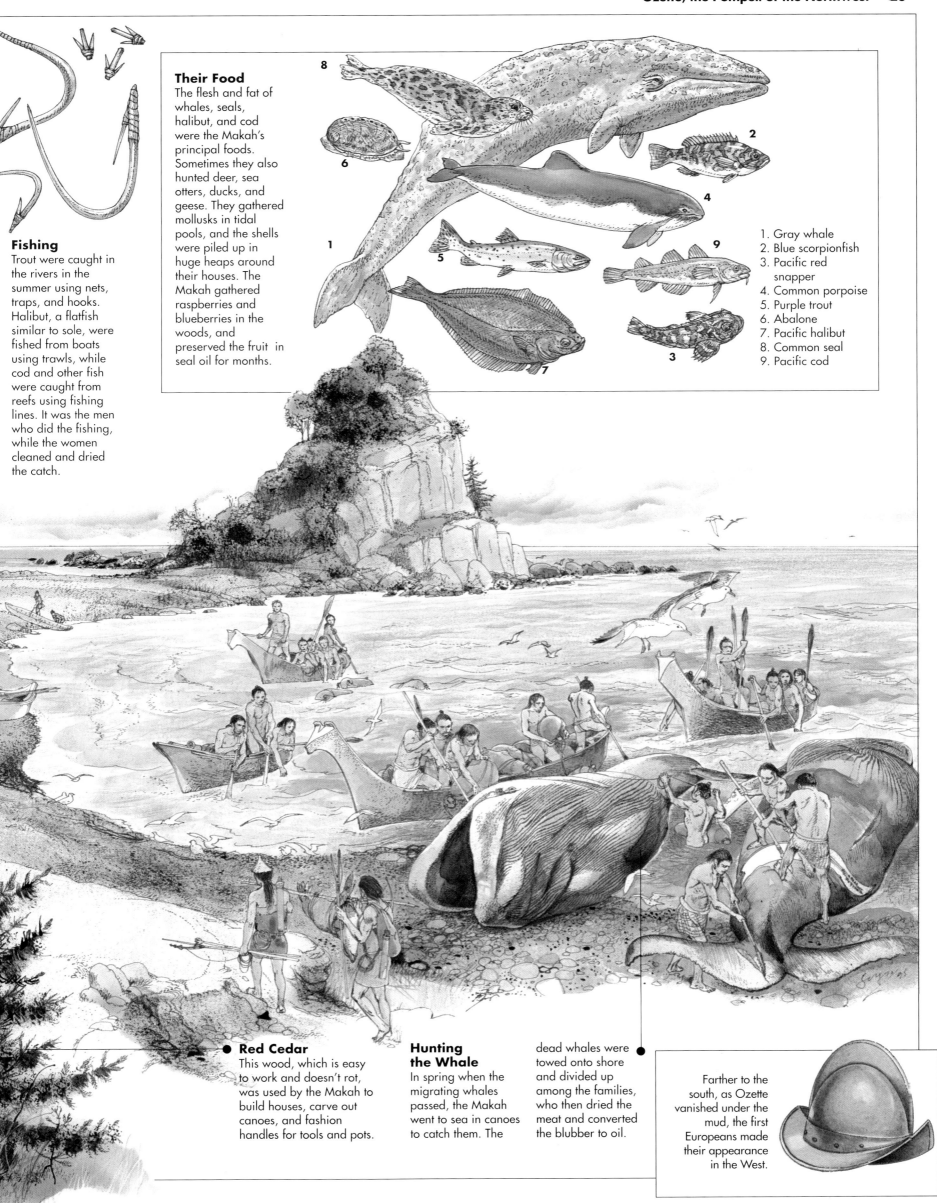

Fishing

Trout were caught in the rivers in the summer using nets, traps, and hooks. Halibut, a flatfish similar to sole, were fished from boats using trawls, while cod and other fish were caught from reefs using fishing lines. It was the men who did the fishing, while the women cleaned and dried the catch.

Their Food

The flesh and fat of whales, seals, halibut, and cod were the Makah's principal foods. Sometimes they also hunted deer, sea otters, ducks, and geese. They gathered mollusks in tidal pools, and the shells were piled up in huge heaps around their houses. The Makah gathered raspberries and blueberries in the woods, and preserved the fruit in seal oil for months.

1. Gray whale
2. Blue scorpionfish
3. Pacific red snapper
4. Common porpoise
5. Purple trout
6. Abalone
7. Pacific halibut
8. Common seal
9. Pacific cod

● Red Cedar

This wood, which is easy to work and doesn't rot, was used by the Makah to build houses, carve out canoes, and fashion handles for tools and pots.

Hunting the Whale

In spring when the migrating whales passed, the Makah went to sea in canoes to catch them. The dead whales were towed onto shore and divided up among the families, who then dried the meat and converted the blubber to oil.

Farther to the south, as Ozette vanished under the mud, the first Europeans made their appearance in the West.

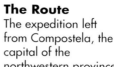

Coronado's Expedition

Coronado
In 1510, Francisco Coronado was born to a noble family in Salamanca, Spain. At the age of twenty-five, Coronado went to seek his fortune in Mexico. There he made a name for himself when he put down an Indian rebellion. He married the daughter of the wealthy royal treasurer, and became governor of Nueva Galicia.

Fray Marcos
Between 1539 and 1540, Fray Marcos journeyed across the Southwest. His slave, Estebanico, had gone on ahead of him with orders to leave a wooden cross behind as a marker if he found any towns that were rich in gold.

In 1539, on his return to Mexico from a trip north, Fray Marcos de Niza told Viceroy Don Antonio de Mendoza about the existence of the Seven Cities of Cibola, with their grand houses covered in gold and turquoise. The viceroy decided to send a military expedition into those unknown lands under the command of his finest officer, Francisco Vásquez de Coronado. The expedition left on 23 February 1540 and headed north across a mountainous region abounding in forests and alligator-infested rivers to Hawikuh, the capital of the Seven Cities. Great was their disappointment when all they found was a wretchedly poor village where they were greeted with a flight of arrows from the Indians' bows. In Hawikuh Coronado learned that the real city of gold, Quivira, lay to the northeast. For three months, Coronado advanced across the dusty plains—vast, empty expanses of grass. But the Spanish didn't find gold in Quivira either. What they found was merely a village of thatch-roofed huts. So the expedition went back home—with no gold, but with the first accounts of the Wild West.

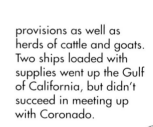

Turkey
When they arrived at the Acoma pueblo, the men of the expedition were given a gift of animals that no European had ever before laid eyes on: turkeys.

● The Route
The expedition left from Compostela, the capital of the northwestern province of Mexico, and headed north as far as Cibola. It then continued on to the east across the Sangre de Cristo Mountains, and finally headed northeast across the plains to Quivira. From there, the men turned back, following the same route in reverse.

● Outfitting the Expedition
When Coronado's small army set out, it numbered 336 soldiers, 1,300 Indian volunteers, and a total of 559 horses and mules for transporting provisions as well as herds of cattle and goats. Two ships loaded with supplies went up the Gulf of California, but didn't succeed in meeting up with Coronado.

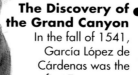

The Discovery of the Grand Canyon ●
In the fall of 1541, García López de Cárdenas was the first European to look out on the Grand Canyon.

Tigeux Pueblo
This was a small village of twelve masonry houses built on high ground. At its feet stretched luxuriant fields of maize, beans, and melons.

The Arrival of the Horse
The horse, long extinct in America, returned to the West with the Spanish. The first three horses ran away from Coronado's men; later on, the Indians stole many other horses from the Spanish missions.

Beams
Tree trunks had been carried from forests in the Sangre de Cristo Mountains.

The Revolt of Tigeux Pueblo
The expedition spent the winter of 1540–41 in Tigeux pueblo, requisitioning food from the Indians. Relations between the Spanish and the native inhabitants soon grew strained, and when a soldier offended a young Indian woman, it was cause for revolt. The Indians drove off the Spaniards' horses and mules, and barricaded themselves in their houses. Coronado's men used smoke to force the Indians out of their houses. Once the revolt had been put down, some of the rebels were tied up and burned alive.

Two centuries later, the exploration of the West was continued by Lewis and Clark.

THE LEWIS AND CLARK EXPEDITION

The American people came to know more about the vast, wild expanses of the West as the result of an expedition proposed by President Thomas Jefferson. The expedition's objectives: discover river routes to the Pacific; draw maps of the territories it passed through; test the fertility of the soil; make notes on the climate, flora, and fauna; discover mining deposits; and gather information on the Indians of the West. The expedition, commanded by Meriwether Lewis and William Clark, set out from the Mississippi River on 14 May 1804, and went up the Missouri River in a keelboat and two canoes. They returned to the Mississippi in September of 1806, having traveled 8,000 miles (well over 12,000 km) across completely untamed territories with a loss of only one man, who died of appendicitis.

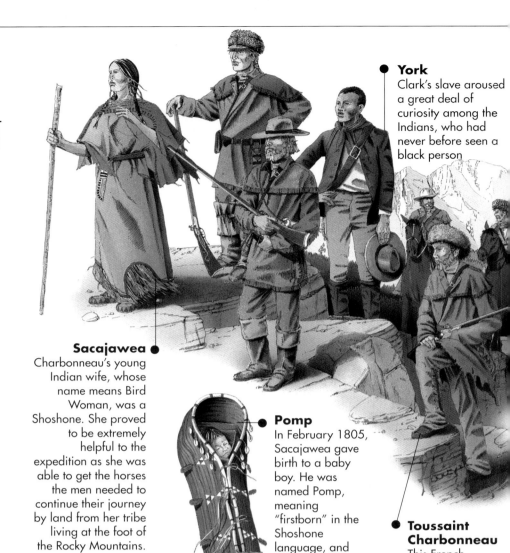

York
Clark's slave aroused a great deal of curiosity among the Indians, who had never before seen a black person

Sacajawea
Charbonneau's young Indian wife, whose name means Bird Woman, was a Shoshone. She proved to be extremely helpful to the expedition as she was able to get the horses the men needed to continue their journey by land from her tribe living at the foot of the Rocky Mountains.

Pomp
In February 1805, Sacajawea gave birth to a baby boy. He was named Pomp, meaning "firstborn" in the Shoshone language, and made the whole journey on his mother's back.

Toussaint Charbonneau
This French Canadian fur trader joined the expedition at Fort Mandan, offering himself as a guide and interpreter

13 August 1805
Meeting with Cameahwait, chief of the Shoshone, who provided Lewis and Clark with a guide named Toby and twenty-eight horses

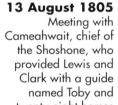

26 July 1805
Arrival at the headwaters of the Missouri River and the Continental Divide in the Rocky Mountains

October 1805
Discovery of the great conifer forests in Chinook territory

7 December 1805
Arrival on the Pacific Coast and building of Fort Clatsop, where the expedition spent its second winter before heading back east

Thomas Jefferson
Third president of the United States, Jefferson served for two terms, from 1801 to 1808. The expedition was his idea, and it was he who chose Meriwether Lewis, his personal secretary, to command it. He also provided Lewis with meticulous instructions.

September 1805
Crossing of the wild, snow-covered Bitterroot Mountains, where the expedition suffered from starvation

29 April 1805
Encounter along the banks of the Missouri River with the first grizzly bear, the largest carnivore in the Americas

November 1804–March 1805
Winter at Fort Mandan, from the name of the Indian tribe who lived in the surrounding area

September 1804
Encounter with huge herds of bison and discovery of the pronghorn in South Dakota

The Prairie Dog
The men of this expedition were the first Europeans to see prairie dogs, which Lewis called "barking squirrels" because of their peculiar warning whistle.

Encounters with the Indians
Encounters with the tribes in the territories crossed by the expedition were almost always peaceful and cordial. The expedition was frequently helped by Indians who welcomed the explorers and offered them food, horses, and guides. Lewis and Clark gave tribal chiefs a medal with a portrait of Jefferson on the face of the medal and the clasped hands of a white man and an Indian on the back.

The Corps of Discovery
The expedition consisted of Lewis, Clark, York, twenty-nine soldiers on permanent detachment, and another sixteen who had been taken on for the first year only.

Game
A few of the men were given the task of hunting game to provide meat for the Corps of Discovery.

Lewis noted in his journal: "four deer, or 1 elk and 1 deer, or else 1 buffalo are needed every 24 hours to feed us."

Meriwether Lewis
A Virginian, born in 1774, Lewis was an officer in the United States Army who distinguished himself in the Indian campaigns. He became Jefferson's personal secretary in 1801. Two years later, Jefferson picked Lewis to command the expedition.

William Clark
Clark was as practical and extroverted as Lewis was idealistic and introverted. In accepting Lewis's offer, Clark wrote: "This is an undertaking fraited with many difeculties, but My friend I do assure you that no man lives with whome I would perfur to undertake Such a Trip &c. as yourself."

14 May 1804
The expedition's departure on the Missouri River in flat-bottomed wooden canoes and a keelboat.

The Air Gun
Not very accurate at long range and not as powerful as a normal rifle, Lewis's air gun did not require gunpowder and it could fire up to forty shots in succession. The Indians called the rifle Big Medicine.

In the meantime, the introduction of the horse had changed the life of the Plains Indians forever.

Hunting the Buffalo on Horseback

The Plains Indians first came into contact with the horse in the sixteenth century when the Spanish began to raise these animals on ranches in Texas and New Mexico. Over the course of two centuries, the Indians became extraordinary horsemen and the horse transformed their life. Nomadic tribes, who formerly had only migrated on foot, were now able to relocate their camps with greater ease. And it was also easier for the Indians to track the unpredictable movements of the migrating herds of buffalo, an extraordinarily important development. For during this same period, this animal had become an indispensable source of food, clothing, and many other articles of daily life. The great buffalo hunts took place in the late spring and summer when the herds gathered to mate. Then the different tribal clans, who were scattered at other times of the year, came back together. Hunting the buffalo was the responsibility of the men, who silently drew to within a few yards of the herd. Unfortunately, there was always a risk that impatient young hunters would scare the herd off too soon. At an agreed-upon signal, the slaughter with bows and arrows began. Then the women played their part and butchered the animals on the spot.

The Sun Dance
The Plains Indians' most important religious festival was the sun dance, which took place in the summer on the occasion of the great gatherings for the buffalo hunt. It began with the slaughter of a buffalo whose hide was hung on the center pole of the sacred lodge. The ceremony continued for at least four days with dances, feasting, games, mock battles, and tests of bravery for the warriors. The sun dance was performed to assure a successful buffalo hunt.

The Tepee
It came into use after the arrival of the horse, which enabled it to be transported easily. Between 10 and 13 feet (3 and 4 m) tall, the tepee was held up by wooden poles and covered with buffalo hide. An opening at the top allowed the smoke from the hearth to escape. Tepees were often painted with religious or magical images, or with heroic deeds in battle.

Their Horses
The breeds raised by the Plains Indians have almost disappeared. They were short horses, with large heads, round bellies, and small hooves, and were renowned for their endurance, strength, and speed.

Fire
Wood is scarce on the plains. This is why the Indians used buffalo dung, which is rich in vegetable fibers, as a fuel.

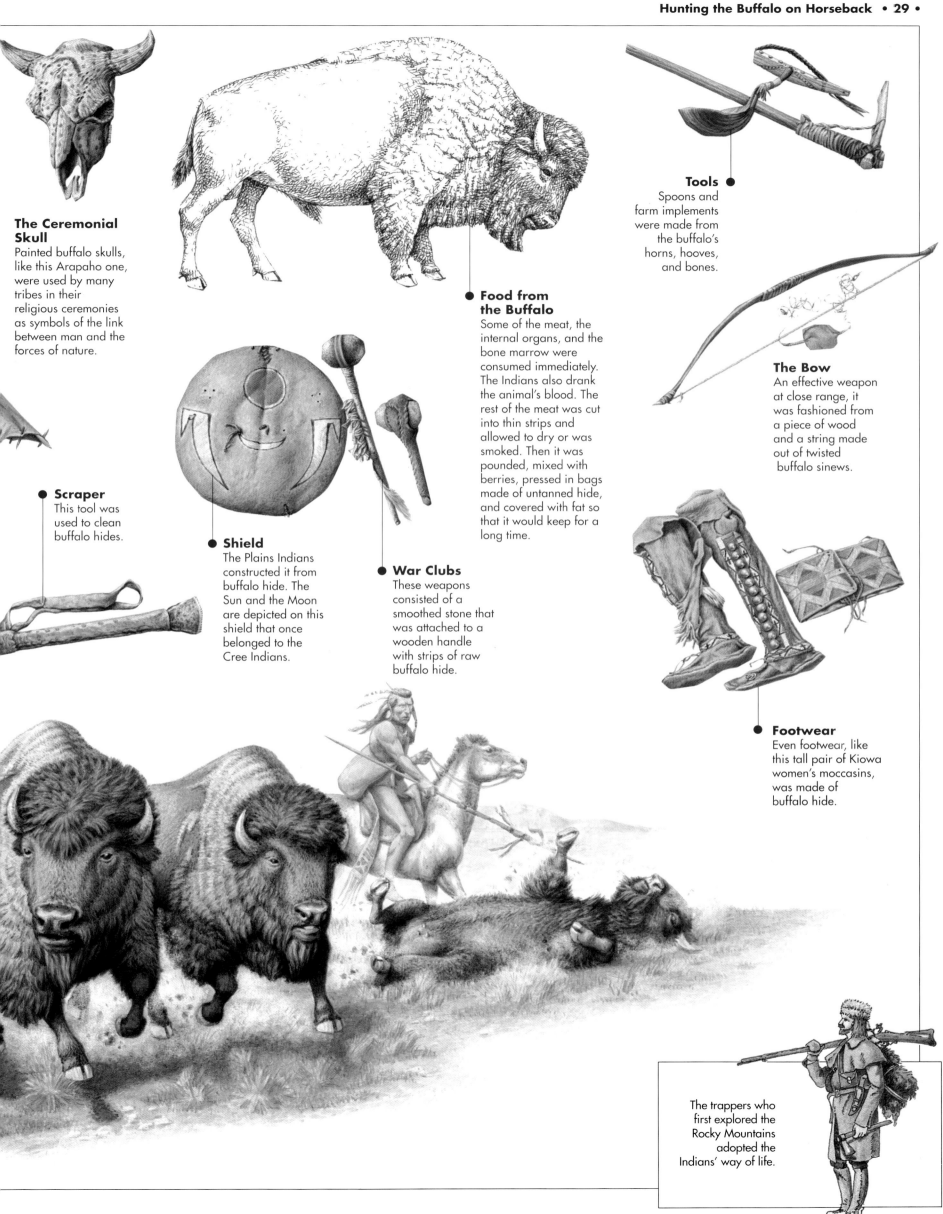

The Ceremonial Skull
Painted buffalo skulls, like this Arapaho one, were used by many tribes in their religious ceremonies as symbols of the link between man and the forces of nature.

Tools
Spoons and farm implements were made from the buffalo's horns, hooves, and bones.

Food from the Buffalo
Some of the meat, the internal organs, and the bone marrow were consumed immediately. The Indians also drank the animal's blood. The rest of the meat was cut into thin strips and allowed to dry or was smoked. Then it was pounded, mixed with berries, pressed in bags made of untanned hide, and covered with fat so that it would keep for a long time.

The Bow
An effective weapon at close range, it was fashioned from a piece of wood and a string made out of twisted buffalo sinews.

Scraper
This tool was used to clean buffalo hides.

Shield
The Plains Indians constructed it from buffalo hide. The Sun and the Moon are depicted on this shield that once belonged to the Cree Indians.

War Clubs
These weapons consisted of a smoothed stone that was attached to a wooden handle with strips of raw buffalo hide.

Footwear
Even footwear, like this tall pair of Kiowa women's moccasins, was made of buffalo hide.

The trappers who first explored the Rocky Mountains adopted the Indians' way of life.

TRAPPERS IN THE ROCKY MOUNTAINS

The Beaver
What drove the mountain men into the wildest areas of the West was the great demand for beaver pelts in the cities back East. Not only used for making clothing, beaver skins were also essential in the production of felt for top hats that were all the rage in the early nineteenth century.

Among the first people to explore the wild Rocky Mountains were the mountain men, fur trappers who often wandered alone for months, or even years, in search of streams rich with beaver. When a mountain man found a bountiful stream, he stayed there for weeks, trapping the animals, skinning them, and drying their pelts. The mountain men led a very free life: They could stay where they wanted to, hunt when they felt like it, or just laze about. The only law the mountain men recognized was the survival of the strongest and the smartest. But theirs was also an extremely hard life. They had to face freezing cold temperatures in the winter, encounters with grizzlies and pumas, and Indian attacks. The men who could endure such a life were without a doubt exceptional individuals and had no desire to go back to the civilized world. Unfortunately, these men were also responsible for the slaughter of hundreds of thousands of wild animals.

The Rendezvous
The sites chosen for the summer gatherings, called rendezvous, were scattered along the course of the Missouri River.

Rifle
More than for hunting, the mountain man used his rifle to defend himself against Indians who believed the whites were poachers.

Powder Horn
It was used as a container for the gunpowder and shot needed to make their own bullets.

Satchel
It held the little things needed for everyday life: a pipe, tobacco, a mold for bullets, and a whetstone for sharpening knives.

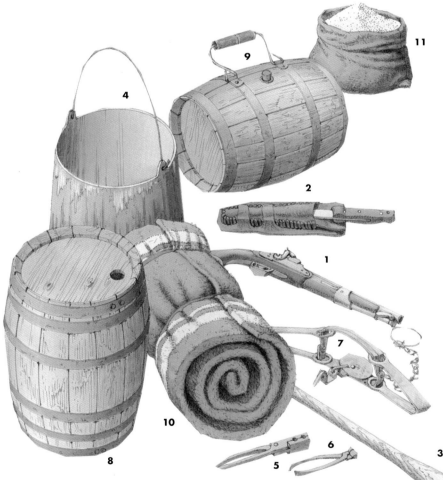

Their Kit
During the summer rendezvous, a mountain man had to buy the equipment and supplies that he was unable to get or build himself. In order to spend at least a year in complete solitude, he had to have: firearms (1), knives (2), axes (3), pots (4), molds for making bullets (5, 6), traps for hunting (7), whiskey (8, 9), blankets (10), flour (11), shot and gunpowder. "Saint Louis whiskey," which was the principal commodity traded at the first rendezvous in 1832, was really a mixture of alcohol, red pepper, gunpowder, and water.

Moccasins
These leather shoes were often purchased from the Indians or made by the trapper's Indian wife.

Fort Laramie
This was one of the trappers' chief meeting places. After having spent a large part of the year without seeing other white men, the trappers came together in the summer for a big rendezvous. And waiting there were merchants who made huge profits by exchanging products from the cities for pelts.

Pelts
Beaver pelts, dried in the sun, were the hunters' principal trade commodity at the summer rendezvous.

Tent
The mountain man moved from one hunting ground to another and spent the winter in a tent made from deer or buffalo hide.

Indian Wives
Some mountain men, having abandoned white civilization, joined bands of Indians from whom they learned the secrets of animals and plants. A mountain man would also often marry one of the Indian women.

The Trap
Beavers were caught with traps that were set out in the afternoon. The traps were placed in the water near the beavers' dams. The bait was made from the secretions of a gland extracted from dead beavers. The smell attracted a beaver which drowned before it could manage to free its leg that had been caught in the trap.

Knife
The trapper always had a knife hanging from his belt as it was an essential tool for skinning the trapped animals.

Jim Bridger
A trapper and guide for troops and settlers for over fifty years

Jim Beckwourth
A famous mulatto trapper, who joined the Crow Indians and became a chief

Over the course of twenty years, the conquest of the West completely transformed communications and the face of the land itself.

CONQUERING THE WEST

Settlement of the West by nonnative Americans began in earnest around 1840. What attracted European immigrants was the promise of land, gold, and independence. For a long time, the vast distances and wild territories that had to be crossed before reaching the "Frontier" were serious obstacles to settlement. Mountain men and explorers had traced the first routes, which soon were transformed into trails traversed by long wagon trains. The heroic age of the West lasted until the railroads were built. The completion of the railroad in 1869 opened up the West to true large-scale settlement, and in the process changed it forever. The arrival of hundreds of thousands of settlers on the hunting grounds of the Plains tribes spelled the demise of these Native Americans who, until 1850, had lived in almost complete tranquillity. Their arrival also changed the destiny of the land itself: The Great Plains were to be transformed into the biggest granary and stockyard in the world.

Stagecoaches — Oregon Trail
Pony Express — Bozeman Trail
Santa Fe Trail — River routes

Smoke Signals
Visible at a range of only a few hundred yards, smoke signals, in addition to messengers, were for millennia the only means of long-distance communication in North America.

The New Travois ●
By the eighteenth century, the spread of the horse had already revolutionized the life of Native Americans, allowing them to relocate more quickly and to transport heavier loads, which they secured to long tepee poles trailing behind the horse.

The Traditional ●
Travois
For thousands of years, the dog was the Indians' only draft animal. A rudimentary sledge, or travois, for carrying baggage was attached to the animal. The rest of the family's goods were entrusted to the squaw, that is, the Indian woman.

The Train ●
From 1869 on, the fast, safe, and economical train finally provided a way of transporting large numbers of passengers and great quantities of goods to the West. At the end of the century, there were 49,680 miles (80,000 km) of track on five lines connecting the cities along the Pacific Coast with the Eastern states.

River Travel
Even before the advent of the paddle-wheel steamboat, rivers had provided the most convenient access to the West. Rafts made from tree trunks were used to travel downstream, but to go upstream, people either used larger rafts towed from the shore or birch bark canoes.

From the Mississippi to the Pacific

Wagon	6 months
Stagecoach	25 days
Pony Express	10.5 days
Train	2 days

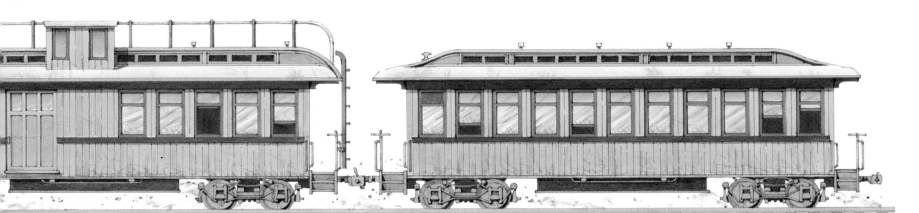

The Stagecoach
In the second half of the nineteenth century, the stagecoach was the most comfortable and fastest means of travel for people who had little luggage and a lot of money. The coach, suspended on leaf springs by long strips of leather, was drawn by two or three pairs of horses and could carry eighteen passengers. Outlaws posed the greatest danger during the trip.

The American Express Company
Founded by John Butterfield in 1857, this first stagecoach service connected Saint Louis and San Francisco. The trip cost $200. The company had 2,590 stagecoaches, 1,800 horses, and over 1,000 employees.

The Pioneer Wagon
Families of settlers who reached the Far West had traveled there in large covered wagons built of maple or oak. About 10 to 13 feet (3 to 4 m) long, the wagon had to carry at least a 3,300-pound (1,500 kg) load of foodstuff, clothing, seeds, and farm tools. The settlers' lack of experience in combination with a hostile environment and often disastrous sanitary conditions made for a harsh, difficult journey. The settlers traveled in trains of dozens of wagons that were easier to defend than a single wagon.

The Pony Express
For nineteen months, between 1860 and 1861, the fastest postal service between Missouri and California was provided by the Pony Express, eighty riders who changed horses at the 190 stations scattered along the almost 2,000-mile (3,187 km) route.

The first people who came to the West were settlers in search of new land to farm.

THE ARRIVAL OF THE PIONEERS

With the arrival of large masses of land-hungry settlers in the middle of the nineteenth century, life in the plains truly began to change. Poverty and hunger drove settlers to leave their homes in the East or in Europe and undertake a journey that could last as long as six months. The settlers' families traveled in trains of dozens of wagons not merely for reasons of safety, but also in order to save on the costs of the armed escort that was essential when venturing into wild territory where the protection of the law did not yet exist. The pioneer's day began with reveille at four o'clock in the morning and departure at seven. They halted for an hour at noon, and then it was back on the road until sundown, when the wagons were drawn up in a circle for greater protection during the night.

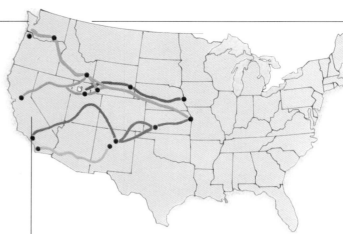

The Trails
All of the trails started at the Mississippi River. The main one was the Oregon Trail—over 2,015 miles (3,245 km), covered in six months. The California Trail branched off from the Oregon Trail. The Santa Fe Trail headed southwest toward New Mexico.

The Homestead Act
In order to encourage settlement in the West, in May of 1862 Congress passed a bill called the Homestead Act that granted a family 160 acres of land for just $30 provided that the family built a house on the land and farmed it for five years. The demand was enormous, but the big railroad companies bought up the best land to sell at a higher price.

What the Wagons Were Made Of
As they had to be both solid and light, the wagons were made of hardwoods like maple, hickory, or oak. Iron was used for the parts that were subject to wear, such as the wheel rims and the leaf springs.

The Wagon Train Master
Before a group of a few hundred pioneers ventured into the wild, lawless territories that they were to travel for at least six months, they elected a wagon master. Chosen by absolute majority, he was owed obedience and respect from all members of the party. It was up to him to settle disputes that might arise among the pioneers. In the case of serious crimes, such as theft or murder, he could appoint a jury charged with enforcing the law and passing judgment on transgressors. Sentences were carried out within an hour.

Food Stocks
Even though the men went hunting during the halts, supplies of food took up most of the available space in the wagon train. The pioneers always carried flour, ham and bacon, coffee, yeast, beans, dried meat and fruit, molasses, eggs, salt, sugar, rice, and tea as well as essential cooking utensils.

Draft Animals
Only the wealthiest people could afford teams of horses for their wagons. More common were teams of oxen or mules—strong, tough animals, but also quite slow.

The First Prairie Houses

During the first thirty years of settlement, houses on the prairies were made of sod, due to a lack of wood, stone, or clay for bricks. Pieces of sod, cut with a plow, were placed one atop the other, leaving holes for the doors and windows, which were closed off with pieces of cloth or leather. The roof was made from small amounts of wood collected along the rivers, and the floor was left bare. However primitive, sod houses did stay cool in the summertime and warm in the wintertime.

Oil Barrel

Hanging from the side of each wagon was a bucket full of oil or fat for lubricating the hubs of the wheels.

The Wagon Load

In addition to food, the pioneers brought farm tools, seeds, alcohol, weapons, and even musical instruments and family keepsakes that often had to be abandoned along the way in order to lighten the load.

But hordes of a different kind of pioneer were also about to brave the journey west.

THE GOLD RUSH

In January 1848, a news bulletin flashed around the globe like lightning: Huge gold deposits had been discovered in California, an as yet largely unsettled area where anybody could make his fortune. The illusion of easy riches was irresistible. At first Americans were the only ones who were swept up in the phenomenon. By June, half of San Francisco had already been abandoned, and by the end of the year, a quarter of the adult population had left Boston. Then impulsive prospectors also began to arrive from Europe, Asia, and Australia. In 1849, 23,000 prospectors, after having braved Cape Horn or Panama, poured off ships arriving in California, while another 50,000 reached it by land after a six-month journey along the dusty trails across the plains. In that same year, almost 288 tons of gold were extracted. In 1852, the year that marked the height of the gold rush, 100,000 new adventurers arrived in California and 2,304 tons of gold were extracted. After 1852, less and less gold was extracted in California, but the hordes of miners kept moving on to the next newly discovered deposit—to places like Colorado and Nevada, forever changing those parts of the West as well.

The Goldfields
In the Sacramento and San Joaquin Valleys of California, 546 goldfields were discovered. In just a few short years, a myriad of towns and mining centers sprang up around them.

Cradle
This was a small, wooden box mounted on rockers in which prospectors, working in groups of three for convenience' sake, could wash about 2,645 pounds (1,200 kg) of pay dirt a day.

John Sutter
John Sutter was a wealthy California rancher who had a small empire of fields and pastureland that he named New Helvetia. It was there, on 24 January 1848, on the banks of the American River, that the carpenter James Marshall found the first gold nugget in California. The news quickly spread to San Francisco and Sutter's lands were overrun by thousands of prospectors. In a matter of a few months, the wealthy rancher lost everything. Years later he was granted a good pension, but he was never able to establish his right of ownership of the gold deposits.

Long-tom
This was a type of long, narrow trough set on a slight incline so that water could flow down it. The prospector threw the gold-bearing soil, called pay dirt, into the trough. Rocks in the soil were held back by a grate, and the sand and gold ended up in a small cradle. The gold was then retained by small rods on the bottom of the cradle. Using a long-tom dozens of yards long, three prospectors could wash up to six tons of soil a day.

Pan
Panning was the simplest method of finding gold. In order to separate gold from the sand it was mixed with, the miner slowly rotated a pan. Working for eight to ten hours, a prospector would only be able to wash 220 pounds (100 kg) of pay dirt.

Industrial Exploitation of the Deposits

Industrial exploitation of gold-bearing lodes started in 1852, when entire hills were gutted, not by manual labor, but by means of specially placed pipes constructed so as to use the force of gravity to generate a powerful jet of water. The gold-bearing soil was conveyed to long-toms as much as 1.2 miles (2 km) long. The environment suffered incalculable damage: Whole forests were destroyed, and with the introduction of hydraulic mining, huge quantities of debris flowed downstream and obstructed the course of the rivers, causing floods and deluges.

Of course, the prospectors needed food, and cattlemen and farmers filled this need.

Trails
Texas cowboys drove the herds along trails that led to the towns served by the railroad.

THE EPIC STORY OF THE COWBOYS

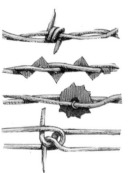

Longhorns
The longhorn cattle of Texas ranches were descendants of cattle imported to Texas by the Spanish missions. Abandoned in arid, uninhabited territory covered with brushwood, the cattle multiplied, reverted to the wild, and developed into large and dangerous animals. In 1860, when the first cowboys began to round them up, about 3.5 million longhorns roamed Texas.

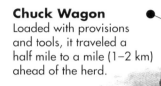

Barbed Wire
Between 1870 and 1874, more and more farmers fenced in their land with barbed wire, blocking the way of the north-bound herds from Texas. Over the course of about ten years, free-range grazing disappeared.

Herefords
At the end of the era of the cattle drive, longhorn cattle were replaced by new breeds like the Hereford, which were not as hardy as longhorns, but yielded the tenderer beef that American consumers of the time were already partial to.

Between 1866 and 1888, the Great Plains provided the backdrop for the legendary activities of the cowboys, men who drove huge herds of longhorn cattle from Texas to the north across 1,500 miles (2,400 km) of savage country. In Texas, where the longhorns ranged free, they fetched three to four dollars a head. But north of Texas, in the cattle towns, they could be sold at ten times that price! And from the cattle towns, they could then be shipped to the densely populated cities of the East and to towns in the West that were gradually being linked to the railroad. The cowboys drove herds of 1,000 to 6,000 animals, with one man for every 250 head of cattle. Cowboys led a hard, dangerous life, for thirty to forty dollars a day. They had many foes—heat, dust, Indians, cattle rustlers, rivers to be forded, and a shortage of grazing land. The heroic era of the cowboy lasted only some twenty years—that is, until the railroad reached Texas and until barbed wire closed the routes across the wide open spaces of the plains once and for all.

Chuck Wagon
Loaded with provisions and tools, it traveled a half mile to a mile (1–2 km) ahead of the herd.

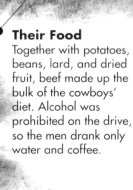

Their Food
Together with potatoes, beans, lard, and dried fruit, beef made up the bulk of the cowboys' diet. Alcohol was prohibited on the drive, so the men drank only water and coffee.

Branding
Each ranch had its own mark that was branded on the animal's hide.

The End of an Era

When Texas was linked up to the railroad, long cattle drives became superfluous. Furthermore, longhorn beef was not very high quality beef, and by the end of the era of the cattle drive, new varieties of cattle had been imported, yielding a better quality of what had become one of the new country's favorite foods.

The Final Journey by Train

From cattle transfer centers, or "cattle towns," like Abilene, Kansas, the cows were shipped by rail to Chicago, and from there to slaughterhouses in the big Eastern cities.

Saddle

No cowboy would skimp on the quality of the saddle in which he spent ten to eighteen hours of his day. Each Western state had its own typical saddle design: The distinctive characteristic of the Texas saddle was its two girths rather than the usual one.

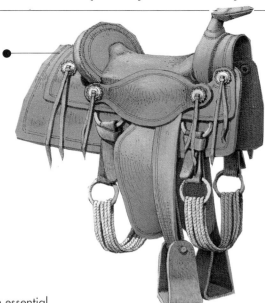

Lasso

The lasso was an essential part of the cowboy's equipment since it was what he used to catch the cattle. Texans preferred a short lasso tied to the saddle horn.

Chaps

Leather trousers worn over the cowboy's regular cloth pants, chaps protected the legs from branches and thorns. The style of chaps differed by region and according to personal taste.

Quarter Horse

Sturdy and fast, it has always been the favorite horse of Texas cattle ranchers.

The Roundup

The roundup was a gathering up of the cattle that had been ranging free during the winter months. The roundup took place in the spring and lasted about forty days. The animals were led to tended pastures or herded to the railroad that would take them to the slaughterhouse.

Cook

Up at three o'clock in the morning to make breakfast, he was also the last one to go to bed at night. And he was not just a cook. He was expected to act as barber, doctor, veterinarian, and, when necessary, even as undertaker.

Markings

In addition to the customary branding, cattle also had marks etched into their hides. A few marks were made on the throat or elsewhere on the neck, others on the ears or shoulders, and a few more below the anus.

Corral

This was an enclosure made from ropes and stakes that was designed to protect the overnight camps from stampedes—dangerous, headlong flights of the herds.

Around the same time as the cowboys were riding the dusty trails, mechanization was making its effects felt on agricultural production.

MECHANIZED AGRICULTURE

The gold rush, which began in 1848, caused a great increase in the demand for agricultural products, a demand that was met by the thousands of new settlers who every year crossed the Mississippi to seek their fortune in the West. And as a result of this great influx of new farmers, in the second half of the last century, fields of grain replaced prairie land on much of the plains. The budding manufacturing industry in the East produced farm machinery, the most famous being McCormick's reaper, enabling farmers in the plains to be much more productive than they would have been using traditional farming techniques. As a consequence, the wheat, corn, and oats grown in the West also helped feed far-off big cities. By the end of the last century, half of all the grain produced in the United States came from the Western states, and surplus grain was beginning to be exported to Europe. Not until the 1950s, with the introduction of chemical fertilizers and pesticides and new varieties of grain, did the United States experience an increase in agricultural production of similar proportions.

The Modernization of Agriculture
From the middle of the nineteenth century on, modern agriculture took hold in the wide open spaces of the prairies. The first reapers had already begun to replace the handheld scythe between 1820 and 1840. And in 1860, they were replaced in turn by McCormick's reaper, introduced in the West in 1848. The cast-iron plow, which had replaced the wooden plow between 1825 and 1840, was definitively supplanted by the steel plow in 1845. Large multiple steel plows came into use beginning in 1890. The first hay-mower was patented in 1847, and the mechanization of the hay-gathering process was completed by 1860. The first grain elevator was built in Buffalo in 1842.

McCormick's Patent
Cyrus McCormick got the original designs for his reaper from the Englishman John Common. He made a few changes to Common's reaper and patented the new machine in 1834.

The John Deere Plow
In 1847 John Deere's steel plow was introduced. This plow was better for breaking up the hard prairie sod than were the old-fashioned English plows.

McCormick's Reaper
Two rows of short, triangular cutters equipped with sharp teeth stuck out from the front part of the machine. The ears of wheat were cut when the two rows of blades moved alternately back and forth.

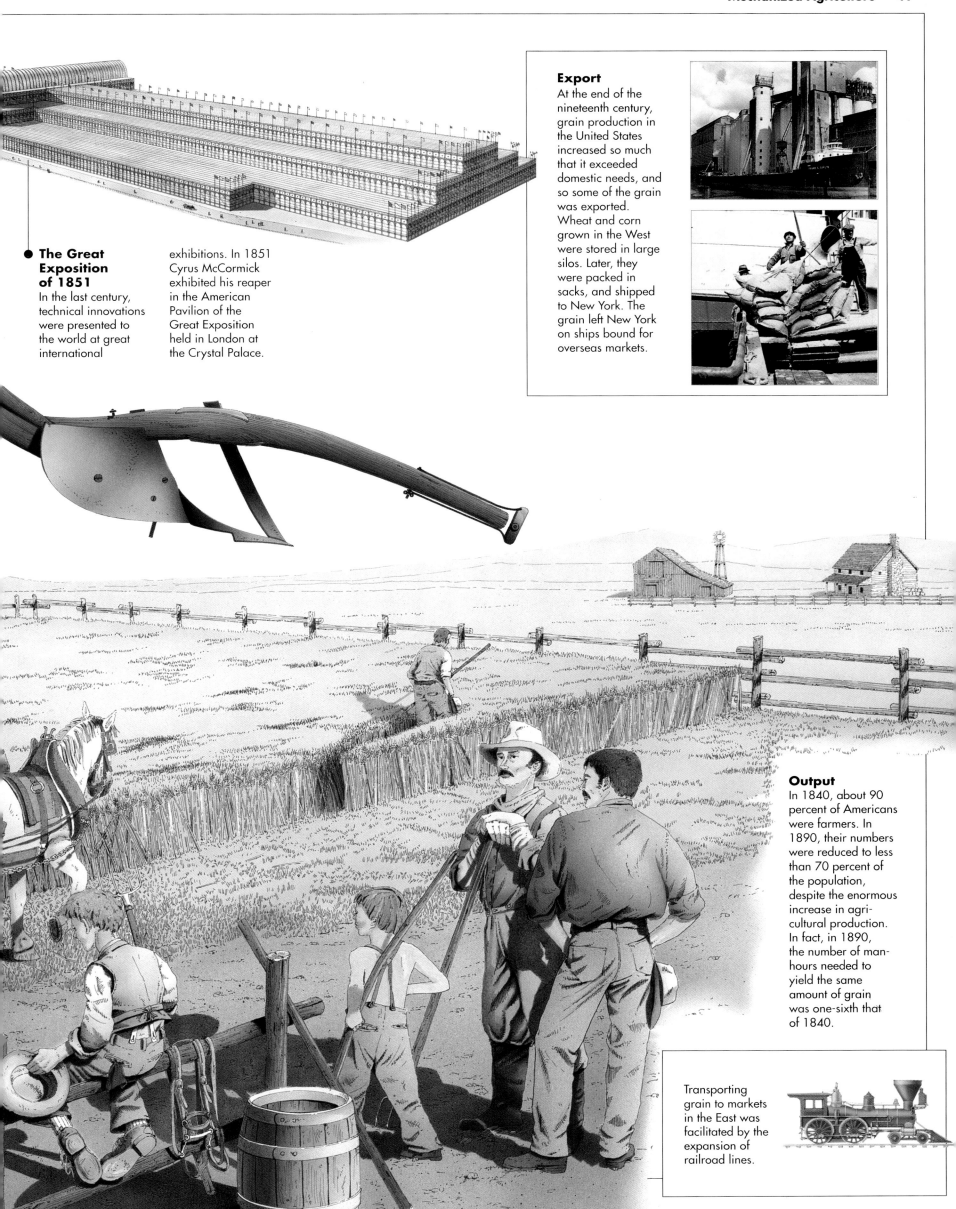

The Great Exposition of 1851
In the last century, technical innovations were presented to the world at great international exhibitions. In 1851 Cyrus McCormick exhibited his reaper in the American Pavilion of the Great Exposition held in London at the Crystal Palace.

Export
At the end of the nineteenth century, grain production in the United States increased so much that it exceeded domestic needs, and so some of the grain was exported. Wheat and corn grown in the West were stored in large silos. Later, they were packed in sacks, and shipped to New York. The grain left New York on ships bound for overseas markets.

Output
In 1840, about 90 percent of Americans were farmers. In 1890, their numbers were reduced to less than 70 percent of the population, despite the enormous increase in agricultural production. In fact, in 1890, the number of man-hours needed to yield the same amount of grain was one-sixth that of 1840.

Transporting grain to markets in the East was facilitated by the expansion of railroad lines.

Theodore Dehone Judah
Judah had already distinguished himself as an engineer while building the Niagara Gorge Railroad when, in 1852, he was charged with the job of tracing a route through the mountains in California.

Grenville Dodge
The Union Pacific operation was directed by Grenville Dodge, an engineer who had made a name for himself as a general in the Union Army in the Civil War and in campaigns against the Cheyenne Indians. Dodge, who received a salary of $10,000 a year, organized the running of his operation with strict martial discipline.

THE RAILROAD OPENS UP THE WEST

Only with the completion of the railroad that linked the Mississippi Valley to California was the West truly opened to large-scale settlement. The train crossed 2,500 miles (4,000 km) of plains and desert and two great mountain chains. How this enormous project came to be completed in a mere five years (1864–69), especially given the era in which it was built, owes much to the fact that Congress entrusted the construction to two companies at the same time—the Central Pacific advancing eastward from Sacramento, California, and the Union Pacific working westward from Omaha, Nebraska. For each mile (1.6 km) of track laid, the company responsible received 10 miles (16 km) of land on each side of the track, plus $16,000 per mile on flat land, $32,000 per mile in the arid Great Basin, and $48,000 in the mountains. Of course, the two companies were competing with each other, and in order to make more money, each company tried to build faster than the other. This haste is one reason why so many workers died building the railroad, especially when they were opening the tunnels in the Sierra Nevada. Many other workers fell victim to Indian attacks.

The Central Pacific
The most difficult stretch of the route, crossing the Sierra Nevadas, fell to this company. Using picks and dynamite, workers excavated fifteen tunnels through granite mountains. The excavation of the highest one alone, which was a good 1,300 feet (400 m) long and renamed Cape Horn, required a whole year of work.

Coolies
This was the name given to the thousands of Chinese workers engaged by the Central Pacific.

Massacre
In the eighteenth century, 70 million buffalo lived on the Great Plains. Relentless hunting reduced their numbers to barely a thousand by the end of the last century. Today they are protected by law, and their numbers have gone back up to about 20,000.

The Buffalo Hunt
The most intense massacre of the buffalo took place between 1870 and 1880. The underlying motives for hunting this animal so aggressively were, first, the desire to free up the wide open spaces for raising cattle and, second, to destroy the main resource of the Indians, whose lands were coveted by ever-increasing hordes of European settlers.

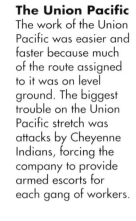

Linking Up

The two operations met at Promontory Point in Utah on 10 May 1869. Two locomotives carried the presidents of the rival companies to the meeting point. In a solemn ceremony, using a silver hammer and a gold spike, they drove the last spike into a laurel-wood tie. The briefest of messages was sent by telegraph: "It is done."

Coast to Coast

With the building of the first railroad across the West, the journey from New York to San Francisco took just six days as opposed to the several months required for a journey by stagecoach. Before the end of the century, a good five lines would connect the Atlantic and Pacific Oceans across the Great Plains.

The Irish

The majority of the 10,000 laborers who worked for the Union Pacific were young Irish immigrants, largely veterans of the Civil War.

The Union Pacific

The work of the Union Pacific was easier and faster because much of the route assigned to it was on level ground. The biggest trouble on the Union Pacific stretch was attacks by Cheyenne Indians, forcing the company to provide armed escorts for each gang of workers.

1600

Seventy million head of buffalo were spread across the plains.

1820

The buffalo had already disappeared east of the Mississippi.

1870

The railroad cut through buffalo territory and the massacre began.

1886

Little more than 830 buffalo survived in all of North America.

Spikes

About 20 million spikes were used to fasten the rails to the ties.

Ties

More than 4 million wood ties were needed to build the railroad.

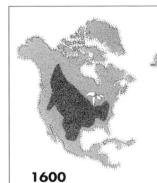

The railroad made it possible to ship dressed lumber for building houses.

HOW HOUSES WERE BUILT

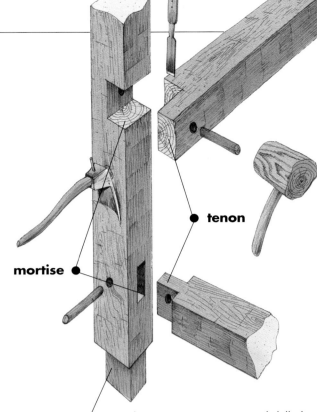

mortise

tenon

The Log Cabin
Typical of northern Europe, the log house was mainly introduced by Swedish pioneers. Even though building a log cabin required a great amount of timber, the log cabin had two advantages: It could be built quickly and it was very sturdy. The chinks between the logs were sealed with clay, straw, or lime. The roof could be made of tree bark, planks, or straw. The enemy of this type of house was fire.

Like colonists throughout history, immigrants to colonies in the New World tried to re-create the surroundings of their homelands. On the East Coast, the English and French introduced the typical building techniques of central Europe: a predominant use of wood for the framework; wood, clay, or bricks for the walls; wooden shingles for the roof. Then, as the United States expanded westward, buildings made of wood spread everywhere, even to regions where timber was scarce. But this proliferation of wooden buildings, combined with an increased need for housing, a shortage of skilled labor, and the development of mechanized sawmills and industrial manufacturing of nails, contributed to the transformation of traditional building techniques into a new method of construction—more restrained in its use of lumber, simpler, and above all, faster.

Mortise and Tenon
The frame of the traditional wood house was based on a system of joints, called mortise and tenon. This method of construction required skilled workers and a lot of time. A few pegs, also made of wood, held the members together; iron was almost entirely absent in this type of framing.

Insulation
Traditional clay or wood walls proved to be an ineffective barrier against the heat. A double layer of boards, one on the inside and one on the outside of the frame with an empty space between them, provided better thermal insulation.

A Sturdy Chimney
The unusually severe climate of North America, with its frigid winters and scorching summers, necessitated a few very important modifications to traditional practices of constructing wooden buildings. First of all, sturdy brick chimneys had to be built to defend against the cold. These chimneys gradually took on the function of pillars supporting the wooden skeleton, and thus allowed builders to construct ever lighter frameworks.

The Sod House
On the virtually treeless prairie, settlers were often forced to build temporary shelters of grassy turf.

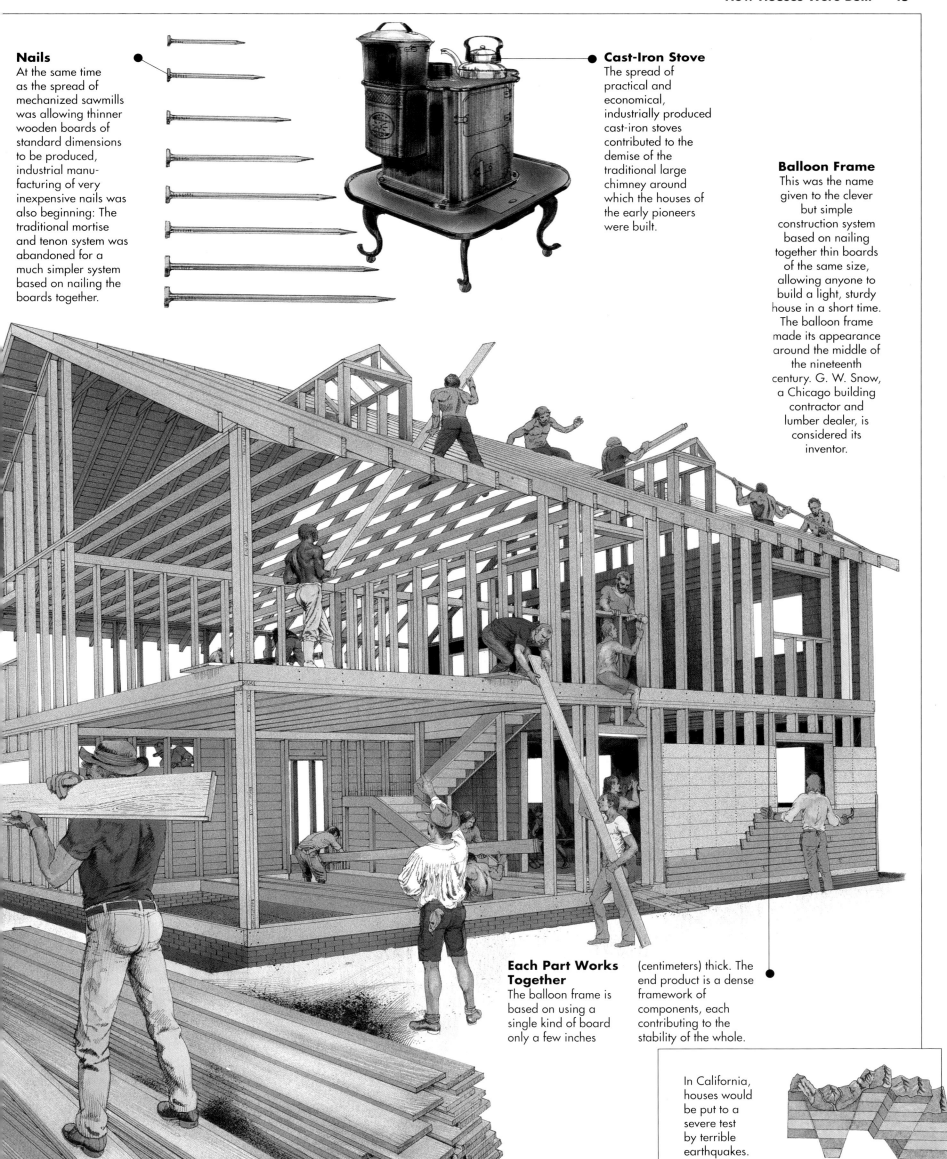

Nails

At the same time as the spread of mechanized sawmills was allowing thinner wooden boards of standard dimensions to be produced, industrial manu-facturing of very inexpensive nails was also beginning: The traditional mortise and tenon system was abandoned for a much simpler system based on nailing the boards together.

Cast-Iron Stove

The spread of practical and economical, industrially produced cast-iron stoves contributed to the demise of the traditional large chimney around which the houses of the early pioneers were built.

Balloon Frame

This was the name given to the clever but simple construction system based on nailing together thin boards of the same size, allowing anyone to build a light, sturdy house in a short time. The balloon frame made its appearance around the middle of the nineteenth century. G. W. Snow, a Chicago building contractor and lumber dealer, is considered its inventor.

Each Part Works Together

The balloon frame is based on using a single kind of board only a few inches (centimeters) thick. The end product is a dense framework of components, each contributing to the stability of the whole.

In California, houses would be put to a severe test by terrible earthquakes.

CALIFORNIA TREMBLES

The Earth Moves
After an earthquake, indications of the movement of the two crustal plates are visible on the surface in plowed fields, on roads, and along fence lines. By measuring the displacement of these "benchmarks," scientists can gauge the magnitude of the movement—in general, the displacement increases in proportion to the increased strength of the earthquake.

San Francisco was already a big city in 1906 when it was almost completely destroyed by an earthquake, a danger that still threatens California. The San Andreas Fault, a gigantic fracture in the earth's crust, passes through the whole southern half of California. Along the fault, the Pacific plate grinds past the North American plate, moving northwest at an average speed of about 2 inches (3–7 cm) a year. In the past 30 million years, the two plates have moved about 600 miles (1,000 km) away from each other. This movement is not continuous, but occurs in fits and starts. As a result of friction between the rocky strata, stress between the plates builds up over a number of years, and then is suddenly relieved through an earthquake: In southern California the earth quakes ten times more frequently than in the rest of the world. According to geophysicists, who constantly monitor the San Andreas Fault, there is one chance in two that a catastrophic earthquake will hit southern California within the next thirty years.

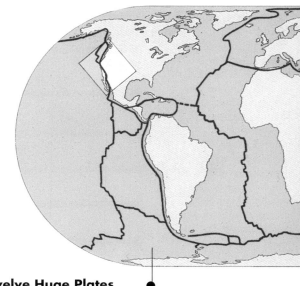

Twelve Huge Plates
The earth's crust is made up of huge continental and oceanic plates.

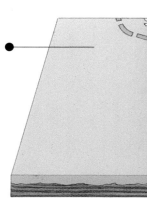

California in 20 Million Years
In 20 million years, the southern California coast will have already become almost an island, connected to the continent by a small isthmus more or less where the city of San Diego is today.

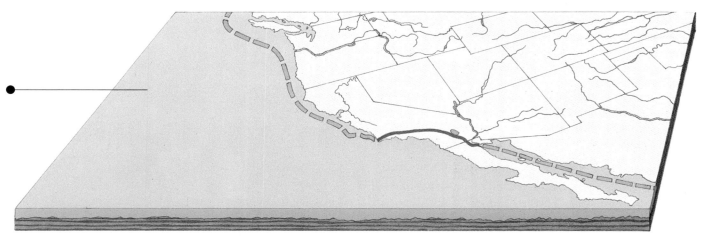

California Today
The southern California coast is part of the Pacific plate that is moving away from the rest of North America in a northwesterly direction.

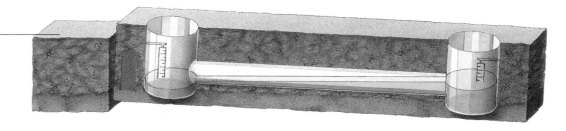

Deformation of the Ground
The stress caused by the movement of the fault gives rise to small dips in the ground near the fracture.

Water Levels
In order to predict an earthquake, the slope of the ground is monitored by large water levels as much as 6 miles (10 km) long. Any shift in the ground changes the level of the water in the containers at either end of the level. The variation can be gauged using either optical or electronic systems.

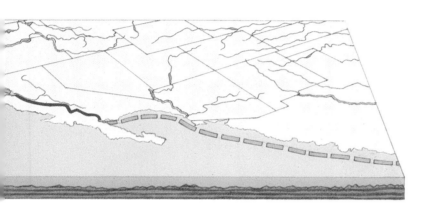

California in 50 Million Years
In 50 million years, there will be a huge new island a few dozen miles off the western coast of North America.

Satellite Monitoring
In order to determine if the fault is moving, the distance between two points situated on opposite sides of the fault can be monitored. Today this is done with laser beams sent from two stations to a satellite that reflects the beams back to earth.

Monitoring on the Ground
A second, simpler monitoring system is one that shoots a laser beam straight to a reflector located on the opposite side of the fault. An atomic clock continuously measures the return time of the beam, reporting any variation in it to scientists.

The San Francisco Earthquake
On 18 April 1906, an earthquake measuring 8.3 on the Richter scale struck the city of San Francisco. Over the following three days, four-fifths of the city, which had been built almost entirely of wood, was destroyed by fires set off by the temblor.

Measurement with an Atomic Clock
Based on the time it takes for the two beams to return to earth—calculated with an atomic clock—geophysicists can measure the movement of the fault.

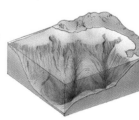

Just off the California coast lies one of the most extraordinary marine environments in the world.

Ed Ricketts
In the era of the great sardine fleets, a man named Ed Ricketts, whose trade was supplying laboratories with animals for research, lived in Monterey. Ricketts, immortalized in John Steinbeck's novel *Cannery Row*, was a legendary Monterey figure. A passionate student of sea creatures, he spent his days working in the rock pools and tidal pools that teemed with all sorts of marine life. Ed Ricketts was the first person to introduce the concept of ecology to marine biology, that is, the concept that the life of an animal can only be understood by taking into account where the animal lives and what other organisms live near it.

MONTEREY BAY

California's Monterey Bay is one of the most extraordinary natural environments of the American Pacific Coast—a submarine canyon 20 miles (32 km) wide and 100 miles (175 km) long with a depth of up to 11,500 feet (3,500 m). There, organisms typical of the open ocean can be found near the coast, sometimes in great quantities. The shape of the seafloor causes upwellings to form that carry mineral salts to the surface, where the algae live. These salts, which normally accumulate on the bottom of the sea, are necessary for the growth of algae. Humans have profited from, and unfortunately also exploited, the biological riches of the bay: At the beginning of this century, a huge fleet fished for Pacific sardines, a very plentiful fish at the time. Fishing reached its height in the thirties. But the fishermen had gone too far, and by the end of the forties, the great schools of sardines had disappeared due to overfishing. Nearly overnight, the fishermen and the workers in the fish canneries found themselves out of work. Today, Monterey Bay is home to a large aquarium and five of the most important laboratories in the world for the study of marine biology.

● Monterey Bay

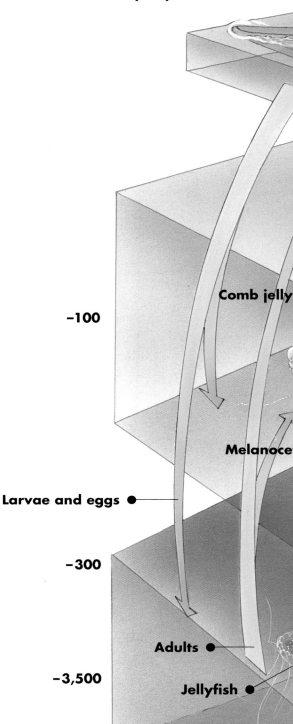

−100

Comb jelly

Melanoceto

Larvae and eggs ●

−300

Adults ●

−3,500

Jellyfish ●

Tripod fish ●

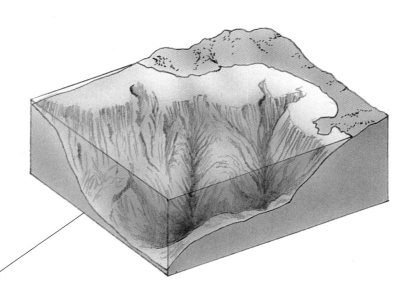

Submarine Erosion
The landslides and mudslides that continue to erode the walls of the submarine canyon are caused by frequent seismic activity, by the weight of the granitic sediments that are found higher up, and by the freshwater that flows out of aquifers.

The Ocean Floor (11,500 feet/ 3,500 m)
The inhabitants of the ocean floor often have long appendages so that they won't sink down into the mud. Many of these creatures feed on the shower of particles of organic matter that falls from up above. Their larvae, however, live in the surface waters, where food is more plentiful.

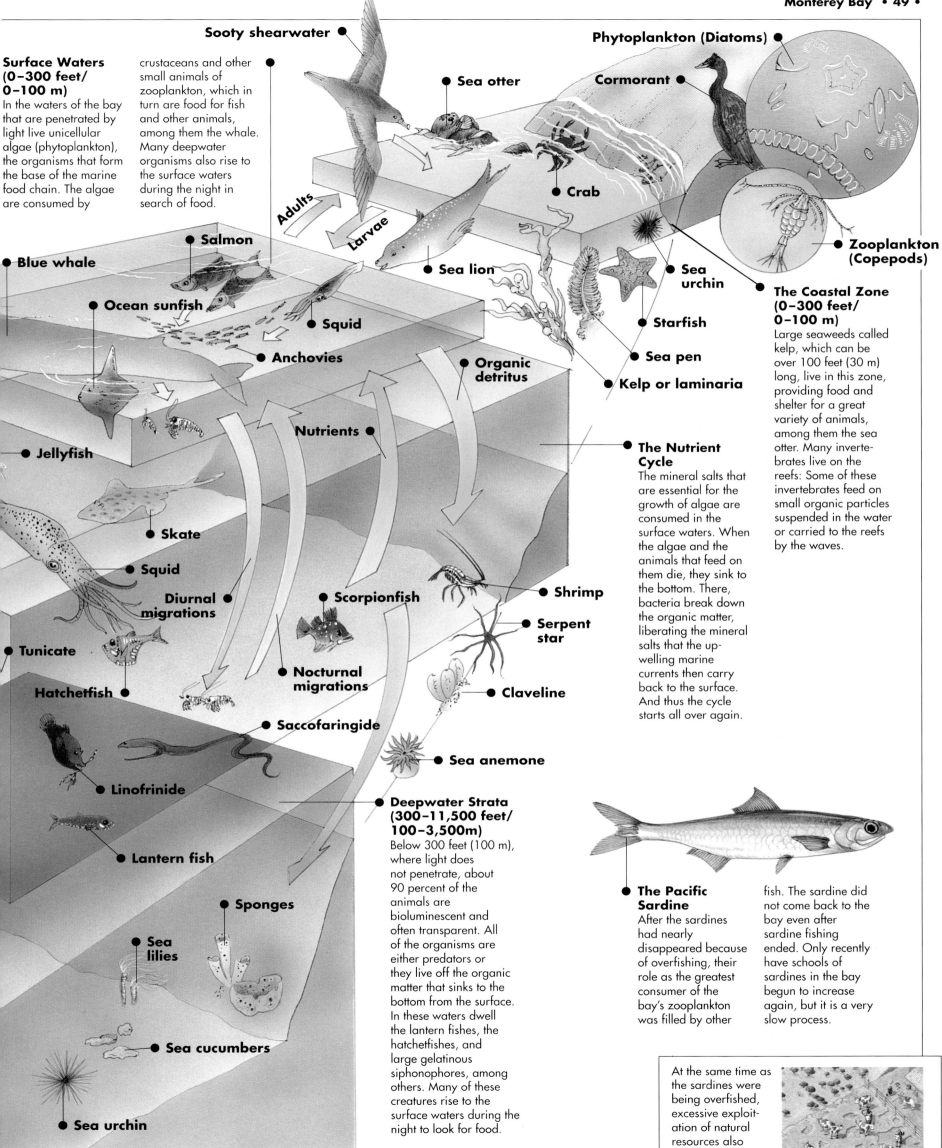

Sooty shearwater ●

Phytoplankton (Diatoms) ●

Cormorant ●

● **Sea otter**

**Surface Waters
(0–300 feet/
0–100 m)**
In the waters of the bay that are penetrated by light live unicellular algae (phytoplankton), the organisms that form the base of the marine food chain. The algae are consumed by

crustaceans and other small animals of zooplankton, which in turn are food for fish and other animals, among them the whale. Many deepwater organisms also rise to the surface waters during the night in search of food.

● **Crab**

Adults

Larvae

● **Sea lion**

● **Salmon**

● **Blue whale**

● **Ocean sunfish**

● **Squid**

● **Anchovies**

● **Organic detritus**

● **Sea urchin**

● **Starfish**

● **Sea pen**

● **Kelp or laminaria**

● **Zooplankton (Copepods)**

**The Coastal Zone
(0–300 feet/
0–100 m)**
Large seaweeds called kelp, which can be over 100 feet (30 m) long, live in this zone, providing food and shelter for a great variety of animals, among them the sea otter. Many invertebrates live on the reefs: Some of these invertebrates feed on small organic particles suspended in the water or carried to the reefs by the waves.

● **Jellyfish**

Nutrients ●

● **The Nutrient Cycle**
The mineral salts that are essential for the growth of algae are consumed in the surface waters. When the algae and the animals that feed on them die, they sink to the bottom. There, bacteria break down the organic matter, liberating the mineral salts that the up-welling marine currents then carry back to the surface. And thus the cycle starts all over again.

● **Skate**

● **Squid**

● **Diurnal migrations**

● **Scorpionfish**

● **Shrimp**

● **Serpent star**

● **Tunicate**

● **Nocturnal migrations**

● **Claveline**

Hatchetfish

● **Linofrinide**

● **Sea anemone**

● **Lantern fish**

**Deepwater Strata
(300–11,500 feet/
100–3,500m)**
Below 300 feet (100 m), where light does not penetrate, about 90 percent of the animals are bioluminescent and often transparent. All of the organisms are either predators or they live off the organic matter that sinks to the bottom from the surface. In these waters dwell the lantern fishes, the hatchetfishes, and large gelatinous siphonophores, among others. Many of these creatures rise to the surface waters during the night to look for food.

● **Sponges**

● **Sea lilies**

● **Sea cucumbers**

● **Sea urchin**

● **The Pacific Sardine**
After the sardines had nearly disappeared because of overfishing, their role as the greatest consumer of the bay's zooplankton was filled by other fish. The sardine did not come back to the bay even after sardine fishing ended. Only recently have schools of sardines in the bay begun to increase again, but it is a very slow process.

At the same time as the sardines were being overfished, excessive exploitation of natural resources also had serious consequences in the Great Plains.

THE DUST BOWL

Rainfall in the plains is unpredictable, and may fall short for many years in a row. But this fact did not stop large numbers of farmers from settling on the plains at the end of the last century. And for a few decades, there was enough rain for farmers to grow their wheat and corn. But beginning in 1933, the rains began to fail. In plowed fields no longer protected by grass, the strong winds that blew across the plains created gigantic dust storms that blotted out the sun for many miles. The first great dust storm, in May of 1934, raised 350 million tons of dust that drifted over the eastern United States and up to 400 miles (600 km) out over the Atlantic. Robert Geiger, a journalist who was present at the time, called the dreadful spectacle a Dust Bowl. And the name stuck. Hundreds of these storms, moving at speeds of over 60 miles per hour (100 kmh) and reaching up to two and a half miles (4 km) in altitude, devastated the southern plains in the mid-thirties, destroying crops and killing domestic animals. In 1938, when the ecological disaster came to an end, 3.5 million farmers had been forced to abandon their land for good.

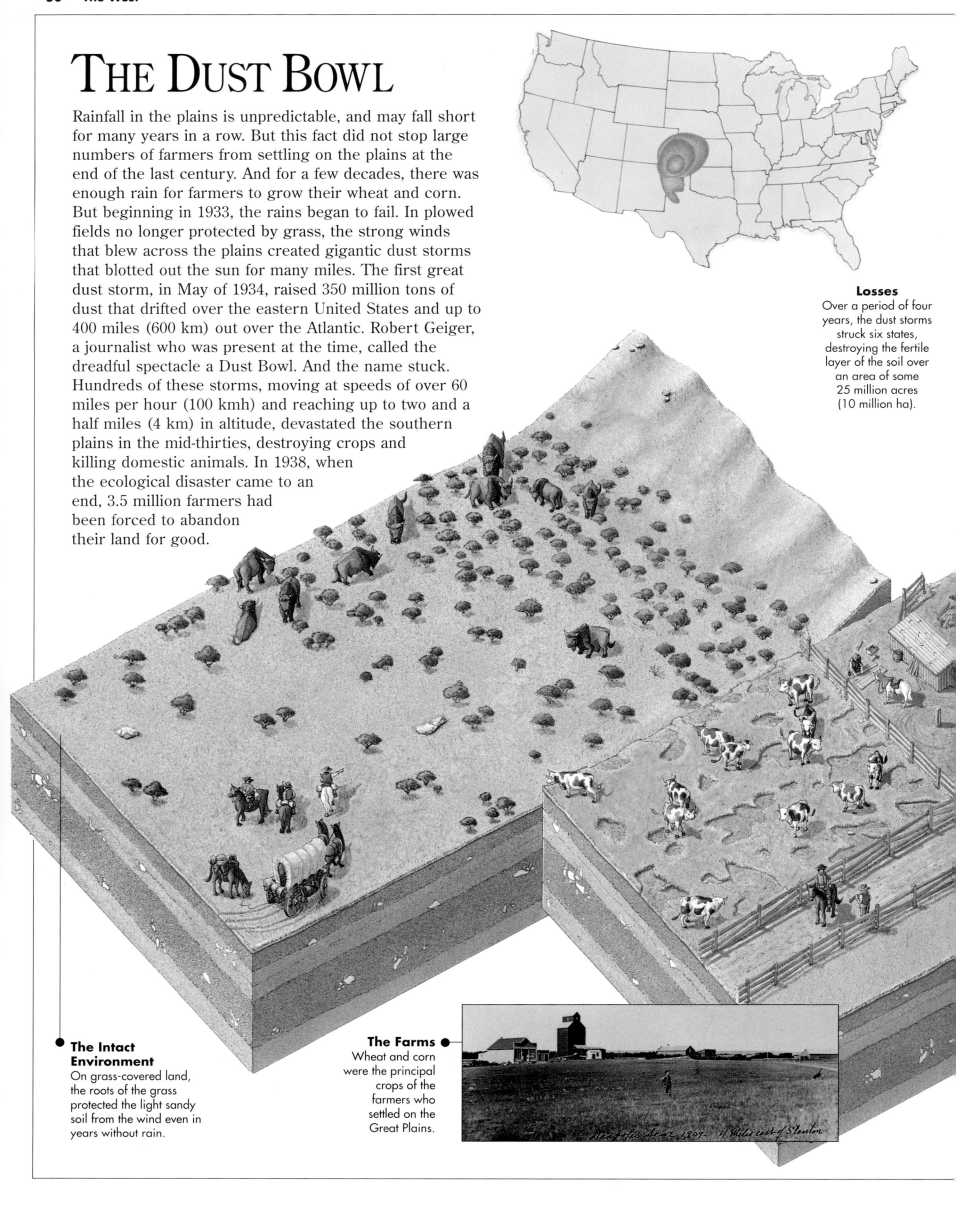

Losses
Over a period of four years, the dust storms struck six states, destroying the fertile layer of the soil over an area of some 25 million acres (10 million ha).

The Intact Environment
On grass-covered land, the roots of the grass protected the light sandy soil from the wind even in years without rain.

The Farms
Wheat and corn were the principal crops of the farmers who settled on the Great Plains.

Photographs of the Disaster

Photographers who visited the stricken areas used a Speed Graphic camera to document the farmers' tragic plight. Approximately 216,000 pictures of the Dust Bowl days are now in the Library of Congress.

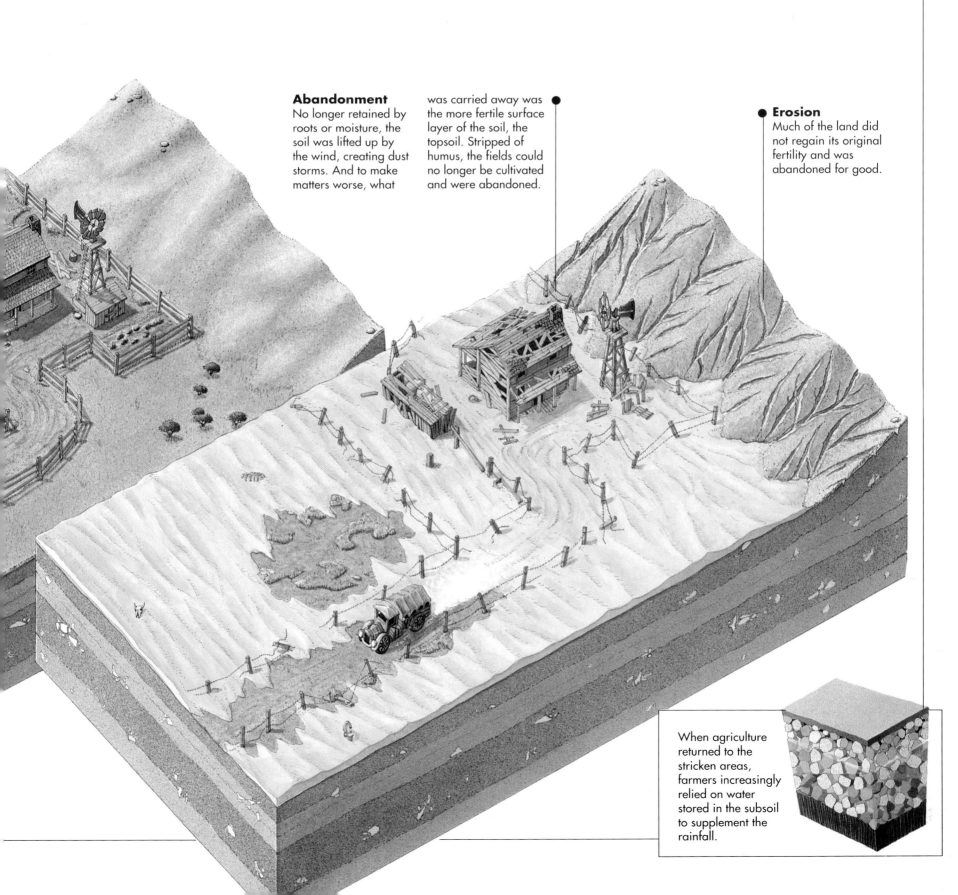

Abandonment

No longer retained by roots or moisture, the soil was lifted up by the wind, creating dust storms. And to make matters worse, what was carried away was the more fertile surface layer of the soil, the topsoil. Stripped of humus, the fields could no longer be cultivated and were abandoned.

Erosion

Much of the land did not regain its original fertility and was abandoned for good.

When agriculture returned to the stricken areas, farmers increasingly relied on water stored in the subsoil to supplement the rainfall.

OGALLALA–WATER UNDER THE PLAINS

After the Dust Bowl days of the thirties, agriculture in the Great Plains began to prosper again. Today, agricultural products from the plains satisfy the hunger of hundreds of millions of people all over the world. The secret behind this miracle is the water held in an immense underground natural reservoir called the Ogallala Aquifer. Rainwater and snowmelt from the Rocky Mountains permeate the ground until they reach a layer of impermeable rock that lies below the aquifer. The aquifer can be easily tapped for irrigation purposes by drilling into the ground and drawing up the water with pumps. For decades, it seemed that the water was inexhaustible. However, today there are more than 150,000 wells drawing so much water from the Ogallala Aquifer that in many areas, the water table has begun to drop to a dangerous level. New irrigation technology and strict conservation measures have slowed down the depletion of the aquifer, but geologists calculate that if it were ever to empty completely, it would take six thousand years for it to fill up again.

Endangered Birds
In several spots, the waters of the aquifer reach the surface, creating wetlands that provide food and shelter for more than a hundred species of birds. Winged creatures numbering in the millions stop for a while on the plains during their annual migration from Canada to the Gulf of Mexico. The lowering of the water table resulting from the continual tapping of the aquifer deprives the birds of important places to rest and replenish themselves. The whooping crane, one of the rarest birds in America, is among the most threatened.

The Biggest Aquifer in the World
The system of underground beds that make up the Ogallala Aquifer lies within the borders of eight states of the American Great Plains and covers an area of about 21,000 square miles (55,000 km²).

Depletion of the Aquifer
Since 1940 the average thickness of the aquifer has dropped almost 15 feet (4 m). And in some areas, like Texas, the falloff is over 100 feet (30 m).

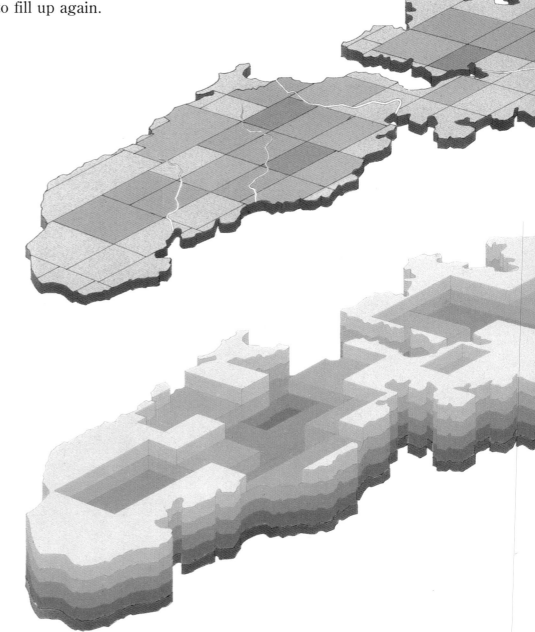

A Huge Sponge
A good way to visualize the aquifer is to think of it as a huge sponge rather than as a reservoir in the usual sense. Water accumulates in spaces between the pebbles and grains of sand in the aquifer, not in a basin as it would in a reservoir. The average thickness of the water-bearing sediment is 200–225 feet (60–70 m), but the actual thickness varies from a minimum of 8 inches (20 cm) to a maximum of about 1,300 feet (400 m). The aquifer may reach the surface, but it can also extend to almost 300 feet (100 m) below ground.

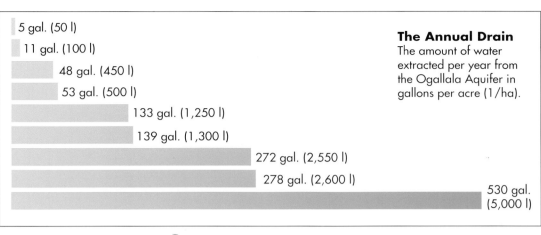

The Annual Drain
The amount of water extracted per year from the Ogallala Aquifer in gallons per acre (1/ha).

- 5 gal. (50 l)
- 11 gal. (100 l)
- 48 gal. (450 l)
- 53 gal. (500 l)
- 133 gal. (1,250 l)
- 139 gal. (1,300 l)
- 272 gal. (2,550 l)
- 278 gal. (2,600 l)
- 530 gal. (5,000 l)

Irrigation Systems

The first systems for extracting water from the aquifer were powered by small windmills. Today, powerful diesel pumps suction over 1,000 gallons (4,000 l) of water per minute. The water is then distributed by large rotating sprinkler arms up to 1,600 feet (500 m) long.

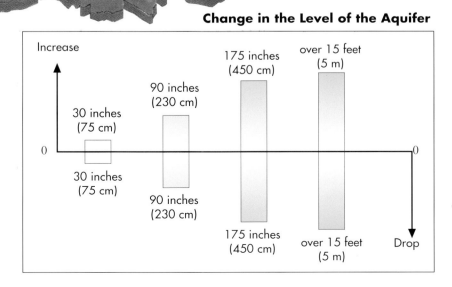

Saving Water

Following warnings about excessive exploitation of the aquifer, a new conservation program was initiated. Today, many farmers are equipped with gauges that measure the moisture in the soil. Thanks to these devices, farmers can accurately determine how much water is really needed and thus avoid losing the excess to evaporation.

Change in the Level of the Aquifer

Increase

- 30 inches (75 cm)
- 90 inches (230 cm)
- 175 inches (450 cm)
- over 15 feet (5 m)

0 ────────────── 0

- 30 inches (75 cm)
- 90 inches (230 cm)
- 175 inches (450 cm)
- over 15 feet (5 m)

Drop

But there is almost no water in the Sonoran Desert, where there nonetheless exists a remarkable variety of fauna.

THE SONORAN DESERT

The mountain ranges that rise along the Pacific Coast prevent moist ocean air from reaching inland areas. As a result, vast deserts stretch across many parts of the Southwest. One such desert is the Sonoran, where scanty rain falls just twice a year, in the summer and in the winter. Desert plants defy this lack of water by producing narrow or spiny leaves, or, like the saguaro, they store water in special tissues. When it does finally rain, the plants bloom and reproduce in a matter of a few days. Despite this harsh environment, many animals have also adapted to life in the Sonoran Desert. Besides water, one of their main problems is the heat of the sun. Different animals protect themselves in different ways: Some are light in color; others stay in the shade or near water holes; yet others have long ears and limbs to dissipate the heat better. Many animals only leave their lairs at night when it is cooler.

Location of the Desert

Saguaro
A gigantic plant, the saguaro can be as much as 50 feet (almost 15 m) tall. Like other cacti, the saguaro has spines that are a type of transformed leaf and a green spongy trunk that retains water and carries out photosynthesis.

Red-Tailed Hawk
A bird of prey that can be found throughout the West, it has even managed to adapt to life in the desert.

Gila Woodpecker
This bird, which is some 8 inches (20 cm) long, drills holes in trees and saguaros. The holes are later used by other animals.

Javelinas
About 3 feet (1 m) long, javelinas are one of the largest desert mammals. They live in groups, and feed on roots, fruit, and tubers.

Blue Paloverde
This shrub has sharp thorns, small leaves, and green tissue in its trunk and branches for carrying out photosynthesis.

Desert Agave
With a fruit-bearing stalk up to 20 feet (6 m) tall, this agave is one of the biggest in the world.

Velvet Mesquite
A small thorny tree up to 40 feet (12 m) tall, it develops very deep roots. Its seeds are sought after by many animals and are also used to make a type of flour.

Daytime
At dawn, the birds and mammals are the first to show themselves. Soon, the reptiles also come out and warm themselves in the sun until they reach their proper body temperature.

Gambel's Quail
A great consumer of seeds, this terrestrial bird only lives in the parts of the desert where it can find water.

Desert Tarantula
This poisonous spider grows to a little over 2 inches (6 cm) long; it hunts its prey on the ground.

Antelope Jackrabbit
Its long ears sprinkled with blood vessels dissipate heat, allowing this jackrabbit to stay cool in the hottest part of the day.

Diurnal Horned Toad
This reptile is about 6 inches (15 cm) long. When caught, it grows stiff and bleeds from the eyes.

Sanborn's Bat
This bat lives in caves in the daytime, and at night it comes out to feed on the pollen and nectar of desert plants.

Great Horned Owl
This is a large nocturnal bird of prey with a wing-span of about 55 inches (1.5 m). It builds its nest in trees or large cacti, and feeds on hares, skunks, reptiles, and birds.

Nighttime
It is only at night that one can truly appreciate the richness of life in the desert. After dark, the temperature drops quickly, and many animals, even quite large ones, leave their lairs. This is also the favorite hour of many predators like the elf owl and the rattlesnake. Life centers around the water hole, and some animals travel long distances to get there, then live off what they have drunk for many days.

Elf Owl
Large insects are the prey of this little owl, which is barely 6 inches (15 cm) long.

Candelabra Cactus
Like the saguaro, this cactus has spines rather than true leaves. Woody vertical ribs inside the trunk support the plant when it is full of water.

Mule Deer
This is a very widespread herbivore, common in all types of environments as long as the environment has an ample supply of food resources like twigs, leaves, grass, and fruit.

Gila Monster
This reptile can be as much as 2 feet (nearly 60 cm) long, and, like snakes, it is equipped with poison glands.

Western Diamondback Rattlesnake
Active at sunset and during the warmest of nights, this snake can reach a length of nearly 7 feet (over 2 m). It is the most venomous of the rattlesnakes and the most long-lived: It can live for as much as twenty-six years.

Roadrunner
It braves the cold nights by lowering its body temperature to 7°C.

Ringtail
This carnivore that preys on reptiles, small mammals, birds, insects, and spiders is about 30 inches (70 cm) long and is particularly common in rocky areas.

In an experiment in the heart of the desert, scientists have re-created a variety of natural ecosystems.

Vladimir Vernadsky

The man who gave the name "biosphere" to the sum of all life-forms on our planet was a Russian geochemist, Vladimir Vernadsky (1863–1945). He was interested in all sciences related to geology, biology, and chemistry. In 1926, he published a book simply entitled *The Biosphere*, in which he expressed the idea that all forms of life on earth are connected to one another and are mutually dependent. They form a single system that is capable of regulating its own functions. In the forties, Vernadsky's ideas inspired the founder of modern ecology, an American named George Evelyn Hutchinson.

TECHNOLOGY IN THE DESERT

Today, the West plays host to numerous centers of advanced scientific research. In one of these centers, a unique experiment was conducted between 1991 and 1993: the re-creation in miniature of a few environments of planet Earth. For two years, four men and four women lived in isolation inside a large, glass and steel, sealed greenhouse called Biosphere 2. The object of the experiment was to study the relationships between different natural environments and test the feasibility of creating self-sufficient communities that could even be used for colonizing other planets. In the over 4 acres (17,000 m^2) of the structure, five different ecosystems were re-created: desert, salt marsh, ocean, savanna, and rain forest. In addition to these environments, a small farm and a micro-city for the eight "biospherians" were also set up. Two large external domes acted as artificial lungs, regulating the atmospheric pressure inside Biosphere 2. The experiment met with some degree of success, but it was not without its problems. For two years, the eight biospherians largely lived off the products of their agricultural areas, and the natural environments were preserved. But regulating the composition of the atmosphere proved difficult, crop yields were lower than expected, and some animal species did not survive.

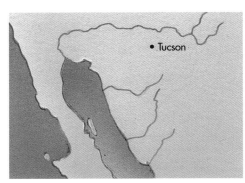

Location
Biosphere 2 was built in the Arizona desert, not far from the city of Tucson.

Biosphere 2
Biosphere 2's facilities were built on an artificial embankment.

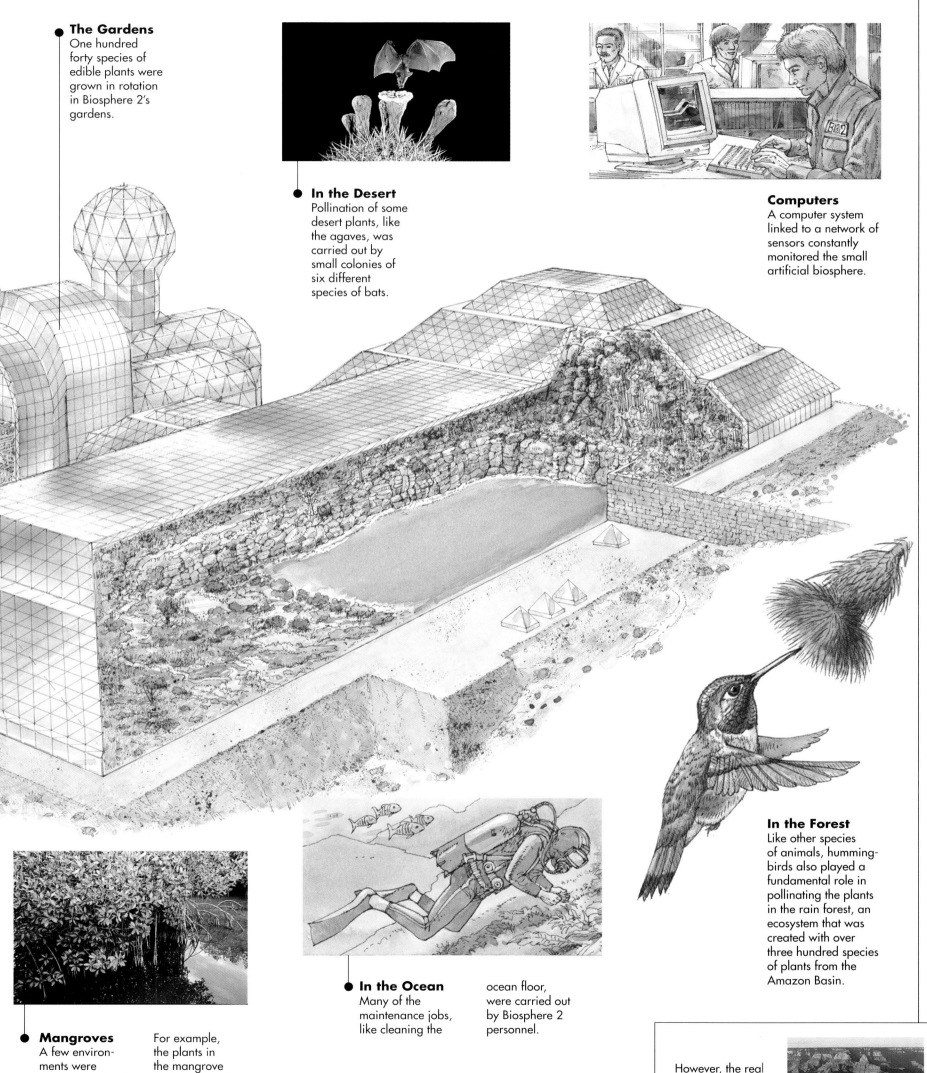

The Gardens
One hundred forty species of edible plants were grown in rotation in Biosphere 2's gardens.

In the Desert
Pollination of some desert plants, like the agaves, was carried out by small colonies of six different species of bats.

Computers
A computer system linked to a network of sensors constantly monitored the small artificial biosphere.

In the Forest
Like other species of animals, hummingbirds also played a fundamental role in pollinating the plants in the rain forest, an ecosystem that was created with over three hundred species of plants from the Amazon Basin.

In the Ocean
Many of the maintenance jobs, like cleaning the ocean floor, were carried out by Biosphere 2 personnel.

Mangroves
A few environments were reconstructed with species native to the United States. For example, the plants in the mangrove thicket were taken from the Florida Everglades.

However, the real biosphere can also be manipulated to meet human needs.

John Wesley Powell

On 29 August 1869, a small expedition completed the first descent into the Grand Canyon. It was led by John Wesley Powell (1834–1902), a man who had no right arm. An explorer, geologist, anthropologist, and writer, Powell attained the status of a national hero with his 98-day journey through the dangerous rapids of the Grand Canyon. In 1878 he helped found the U.S. Geological Survey and later became its second director. Powell was not only the person with the deepest knowledge of the Colorado River as it was in the nineteenth century; he was also able to predict its future. He realized that development of the southwestern states was dependent on water from the Colorado, and he drew up the first plans for exploiting the river. But he also indicated how to make this development compatible with protecting the environment and beauty of the region. Although his ideas were not heeded in his own day because he was too far ahead of his time, they eventually became, and still are, a source of inspiration for people who are concerned about the Colorado.

THE COLORADO RIVER

No other river in the world has carved as many deep canyons as has the Colorado. Nor has any other river been so heavily controlled and utilized. The river cuts through semiarid areas where water is the most precious commodity. Because water in the intermontane West is so scarce, a 1922 law allotted a share of the Colorado's water to each state in the region. Since then, dams, canals, and aqueducts have been built along its almost 1,440-mile (2,320 km) course. They supply water and power to 21 million people all over the southwestern United States, even in cities as far away as Los Angeles, Denver, and Phoenix. Some of the Colorado's water is also lost to evaporation, especially off the surface of its man-made lakes. And so by the time the Colorado reaches the Gulf of California, it has been reduced to a mere trickle, and its delta region, once rich in animal and plant life, is now a desert.

Tourism
The Grand Canyon and Lakes Mead and Powell—vast man-made lakes created by the Hoover and Glen Canyon Dams—attract millions of tourists to the banks of the Colorado every year.

Las Vegas Aqueduct ●
(–almost 50 million gallons)

Hoover Dam ●

Colorado Aqueduct ●
(–over 56 million gallons)

Evaporation from Lakes Havasu and Mojave ●
(–almost 14.5 million gallons)

Davis Dam ●

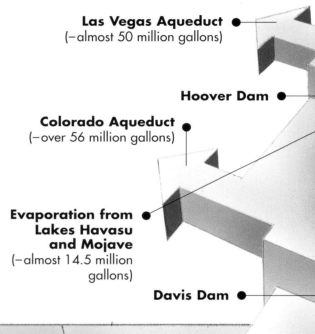

N E V A D A

Palm Springs Aqueduct ●
(–almost 400 million gallons)

C A L I F O R N I A

Mexico Aqueduct ●
(–over 500 million gallons)

● **Parker Dam**

● **Imperial Dam**

Mouth of the Colorado

M E X I C O

● **Irrigation**
The waters of the Colorado irrigate over 12.4 million acres (5 million ha) of farmland in seven states. The water is drawn in the upper reaches of the basin. In the lower reaches, it is too salty and would pollute the fields, destroying the crops.

WHERE DOES THE WATER GO?

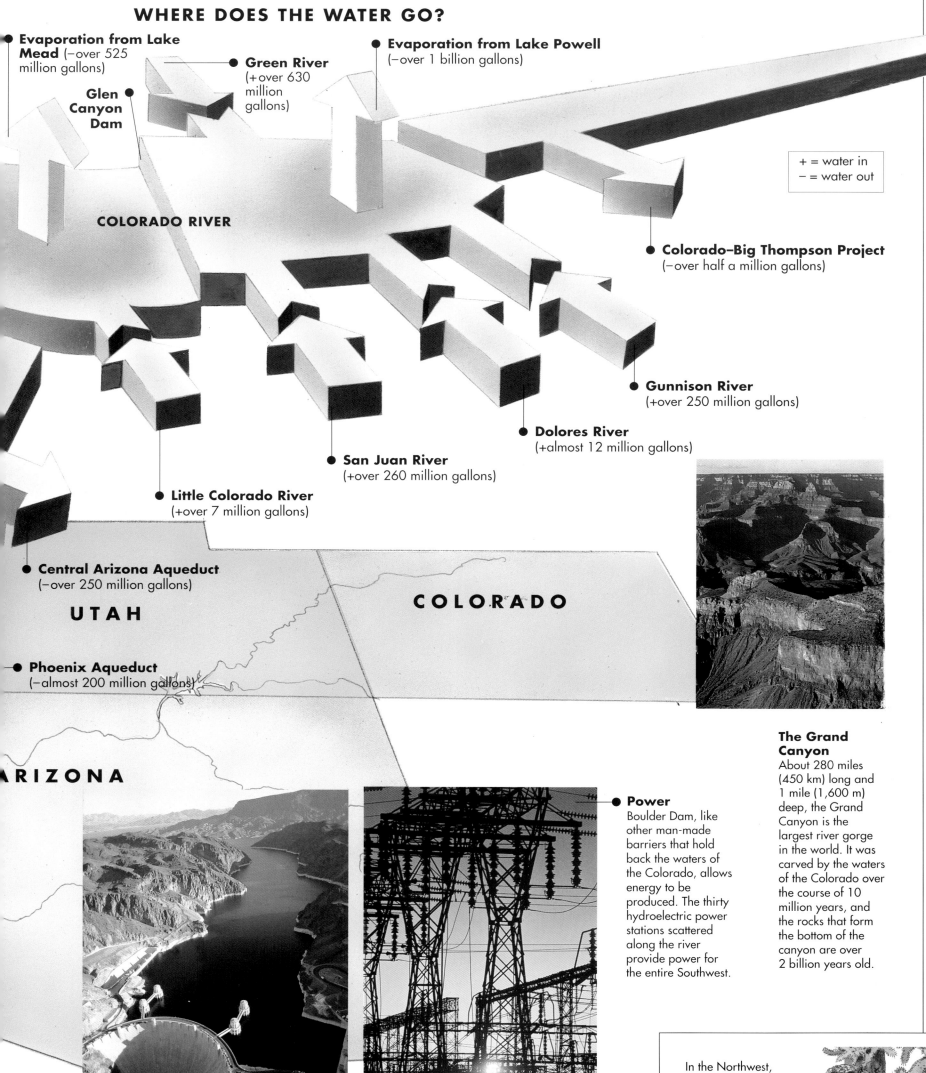

Evaporation from Lake Mead (−over 525 million gallons)

Green River (+over 630 million gallons)

Glen Canyon Dam

Evaporation from Lake Powell (−over 1 billion gallons)

+ = water in
− = water out

COLORADO RIVER

Colorado–Big Thompson Project (−over half a million gallons)

Gunnison River (+over 250 million gallons)

Dolores River (+almost 12 million gallons)

San Juan River (+over 260 million gallons)

Little Colorado River (+over 7 million gallons)

Central Arizona Aqueduct (−over 250 million gallons)

UTAH

COLORADO

Phoenix Aqueduct (−almost 200 million gallons)

ARIZONA

Power
Boulder Dam, like other man-made barriers that hold back the waters of the Colorado, allows energy to be produced. The thirty hydroelectric power stations scattered along the river provide power for the entire Southwest.

The Grand Canyon
About 280 miles (450 km) long and 1 mile (1,600 m) deep, the Grand Canyon is the largest river gorge in the world. It was carved by the waters of the Colorado over the course of 10 million years, and the rocks that form the bottom of the canyon are over 2 billion years old.

In the Northwest, water—not from rivers but from precipitation—gives rise to luxuriant forests.

RESCUED FORESTS

Since Europeans first arrived in North America, 95 percent of native American forests have been felled. Precious strips of these ancient, untouched forests have been preserved in the chilly, humid Northwest where, thanks to the abundant rainfall, gigantic conifers up to 300 feet (90 m) tall still grow today. Hundreds of species of plants and animals live in the shade of these huge trees. Only very rarely has the millennial peace of these forests been disturbed by landslides, storms, or fires ignited by lightning. Despite the exceptional importance of these last forests of the Northwest, up until 1990, they were in danger of being destroyed by loggers and their chain saws. But in that year, the spotted owl was discovered in these forests. This extremely rare bird, not unlike other species of these forests, could not live in any other environment. And each pair of spotted owls needs a good 2,000 acres (900 ha) of virgin forest. United States law now protects animals that are threatened with extinction, so all new logging has been halted since 1990.

Wooded Coastlines
Coniferous forests have been preserved along the northern California, Oregon, and Washington coasts.

Spotted Owl
An extremely rare nocturnal bird of prey, it only lives in mature forests, where it makes its nest in cavities in trees or atop broken tree trunks.

Bald Eagle
The national bird of the United States, it lives in the areas nearest the coast. Its numbers are diminishing due to pesticide use.

Bobcat
A solitary cat, it hunts squirrels and small rodents, and even climbs high up into the trees to catch them.

Grizzly Bear
This is the largest carnivorous mammal of the forest, with a length from snout to tail of over 8 feet (2.5 m). In spring, it easily catches the salmon that are headed upstream.

Pacific Tree Frog
This amphibian is very widespread in the coniferous forests of the West. It hides in moist underbrush and in pools of water.

Red Cedar
This tree is very heavily exploited because its wood is easy to work with.

Pileated Woodpecker
This woodpecker preys on insects and larvae that live underneath the bark of trees.

Wolverine
A fast, extremely agile carnivore, it attacks both large and small animals.

Crossbill
This bird has a sturdy hooked beak that it uses to break open pinecones and extract the seeds.

The Trees
The tallest tree in the forest is the Douglas fir, mature specimens of which can grow up to 300 feet (90 m) tall.

Wapiti (American Elk)
Widespread in Northwest Coast forests, the wapiti is a subspecies of the North American deer.

Life in Fallen Trees
Old, fallen tree trunks provide refuge for red voles and for many species of ants, termites, and beetles. The wood is slowly broken down by fungi, thus returning the nutrients in the wood to the soil to help new trees grow.

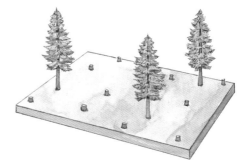

Cutting Down the Forest
When a mature forest is felled, loggers are cutting down very old trees—on average, five hundred years old.

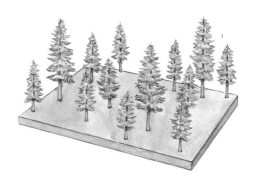

The Young Forest
Twenty or thirty years after the original felling, young trees begin to grow back. After another thirty years, their foliage meets and creates shade in the undergrowth.

The Mature Forest
At least 100 to 150 years, depending on the species, are required for a felled forest to become a new mature forest whose trees will again be able to survive for many centuries to come.

Preservation of these forests is one of the most recent efforts in the policy of protecting nature in the West.

PROTECTING NATURE

The American West was one of the last large areas of the world to be transformed by the hand of man, but it was also one of the first in which nature was protected. The first national park in the world, Yellowstone, was established in 1872. At the end of the last century, a few explorers, scientists, and poets, struck by the beauty of the Western landscape, attempted to persuade the American people of the need to preserve intact at least some small part of those vast untamed areas. They argued that the wilderness should not be disturbed except to study its plants and animals or to immerse oneself in the solitude of nature. These individuals asked, as none before them had, to protect nature purely for its own sake. Their efforts were successful, and from that time on, the number of protected areas has never stopped growing. By the middle of the 1990s, there were over fifty federally protected areas in the West, including national parks, monuments, and preserves.

Aldo Leopold
In the early years of this century, a very young Aldo Leopold, the philosopher of the natural preservation movement in the United States, went to then still-untamed New Mexico to study its plants and animals. Over the next few years, he saw the entire face of the continent transformed in the wake of advancing civilization. From then until his death in 1948, he strove to define a new ethic to govern the relationship between man and nature.

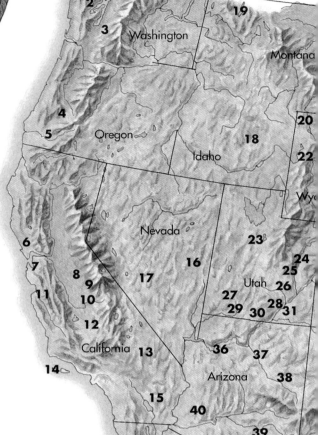

Hummingbird
This tiny bird plays a fundamental role in the pollination of plants in the rain forest.

Giant Sequoia
In the nineteenth century, whole forests of sequoias—the most massive trees in the world—were decimated in the mountains of California. Today, sequoias are protected by law and have become one of the symbols of the West.

John Muir
Muir was a naturalist, mountain climber, explorer, and writer, but is best remembered as a crusader for the preservation of the western wilderness for the almost mystic zeal with which he pursued this effort. He divided his time between the mountains and his books and lectures devoted to making people aware of the enchantment of the places he loved. To him, more than to any other, must go the credit for having convinced the United States to create the national parks.

California Condor
In 1986, when the San Diego Zoo tried to breed condors, only three of these birds survived in the wild, and twenty others lived in various zoos. In 1992, their numbers had increased to about a hundred, and a few pairs have been reintroduced in protected areas.

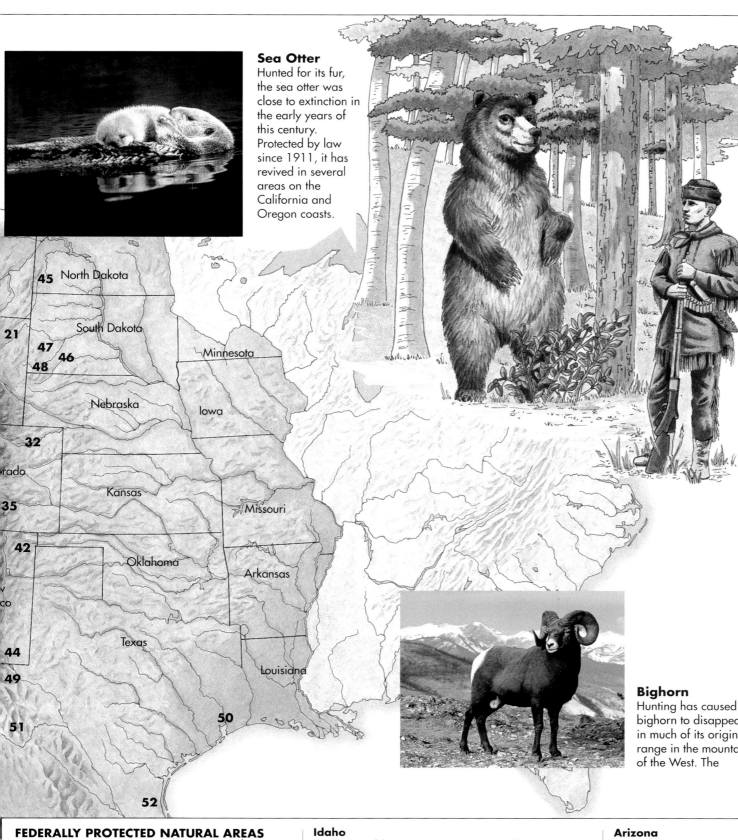

Sea Otter
Hunted for its fur, the sea otter was close to extinction in the early years of this century. Protected by law since 1911, it has revived in several areas on the California and Oregon coasts.

Theodore Roosevelt
Before becoming the twenty-fifth president of the United States, Theodore Roosevelt was an explorer, a naturalist, and a writer who made lengthy trips through the wildest parts of Africa and South America. More than any other American president, Theodore Roosevelt committed himself to protecting nature in the West, due in part to the influence of John Muir, who accompanied Roosevelt on a historic journey to the Yosemite Valley. During his presidency (1901–09), the system of national parks and preserves grew by a good 193 million acres (78 million ha), more than double the 89 million acres (36 million ha) placed under protection by all his predecessors combined.

Bighorn
Hunting has caused the bighorn to disappear in much of its original range in the mountains of the West. The remaining population is concentrated in a few large national parks where, however, they still fall victim to poachers.

FEDERALLY PROTECTED NATURAL AREAS

Washington
1. North Cascades (1968) — National Park
2. Olympic (1938) — National Park
3. Mount Rainier (1899) — National Park

Oregon
4. Crater Lake (1902) — National Park
5. Oregon Caves — National Monument

California
6. Point Reyes — National Seashore
7. Muir Woods — National Monument
8. Yosemite (1890) — National Park
9. Devils Postpile — National Monument
10. Kings Canyon (1890) — National Park
11. Pinnacles — National Monument
12. Sequoia (1890) — National Park
13. Death Valley — National Monument
14. Channel Islands (1980) — National Park
15. Joshua Tree — National Monument

Nevada
16. Great Basin (1986) — National Park
17. Lehman Caves — National Monument

Idaho
18. Craters of the Moon — National Monument

Montana
19. Glacier (1910) — National Park

Wyoming
20. Yellowstone (1872) — National Park
21. Devils Tower — National Monument
22. Grand Teton (1929) — National Park

Utah
23. Timpanogos Cave — National Monument
24. Arches (1971) — National Park
25. Canyonlands (1964) — National Park
26. Capitol Reef (1971) — National Park
27. Cedar Breaks — National Monument
28. Bryce Canyon (1924) — National Park
29. Zion (1919) — National Park
30. Rainbow Bridge — National Monument
31. Natural Bridges — National Monument

Colorado
32. Rocky Mountains (1915) — National Park
33. Colorado — National Monument
34. Black Canyon of the Gunnison — National Monument
35. Great Sand Dunes — National Monument

Arizona
36. Grand Canyon (1919) — National Park
37. Sunset Crater — National Monument
38. Petrified Forest (1962) — National Park
39. Organ Pipe Cactus — National Monument
40. Saguaro — National Monument
41. Chiricahua — National Monument

New Mexico
42. Capulin Mountain — National Monument
43. White Sands — National Monument
44. Carlsbad Caverns (1930) — National Park

North Dakota
45. Theodore Roosevelt (1978) — National Park

South Dakota
46. Jewel Cave — National Monument
47. Wind Cave (1903) — National Park
48. Badlands (1939) — National Park

Texas
49. Guadalupe Mountains (1972) — National Park
50. Big Thicket — National Preserve
51. Big Bend (1944) — National Park
52. Padre Island — National Seashore

• Index •

[Abbreviations: *t*, top; *b*, bottom; *c*, center; *r*, right; *l*, left]

The unpublished and original illustrations contained in this volume were carried out at the suggestion and under the editorial supervision of DoGi s.r.l., which holds the copyright.
Illustrations by: Alessandro Bartolozzi (6 *tl*; 6 *cl*; 6 *bl*; 7 *tr*; 16 *tr*; 18 *b*; 20 *t*; 24 *tr*; 48–49; 58–59) Simone Boni (40–41 *tc*); Giuliano Fornari (4–5; 6–7; 14–15; 62–63); L. R. Galante (16–17); Paola Holguin (29 *br*; 43 *br*; 45 *br*; 62 *cl*); Sandro Rabatti (1; 3 *c*; 3 *b*; 5 *t*; 5 *b*; 6 *tr*; 6 *bl*; 6 *br*; 7 *bl*; 8–9; 10–11; 12–13; 16 *bl*; 18–19; 22

tr; 24–25; 28–29; 30–31; 32–33; 34–35; 36–37; 38–39; 42–43); Sebastiano Ranchetti (53 *tl*; 53 *bl*); Andrea Ricciardi (3 *t*; 11 *cr*; 14 *bc*; 15 *br*; 20–21; 26–27; 33 *t*; 40–41; 46–47; 52–53); Claudia Saraceni (7 *tl*; 7 *tc*; 7 *br*; 10 *tl*; 14 *tr*; 14 *cl*; 14 *bl*; 14 *br*; 15 *tr*; 15 *c*; 15 *bl*; 15 *bc*; 18 *b*; 20 *bl*; 22 *tl*; 24 *tl*; 24 *cl*; 25 *b* 26 *b*; 27 *cr*; 36 *cl*; 42 *tl*; 42 *cl*; 48 *tl*; 56 *tl*; 58 *tl*; 62 *cl*); Sergio (22–23; 33 *br*; 44–45); Thomas Trojer (7 *c*; 14 *cr*; 16 *tl*; 18 *tl*; 33 *bc*; 50–51).
Cover: Sandro Rabatti
Photographs by: Panda Photo (19); Panda Photo/Austing (62 *b*); Panda Photo/Bardi (57 *b*; 59 *c*); Panda

Photo/Calegari (24 *t*); Panda Photo/Foott (4 *tr*; 52; 58 *t*); Panda Photo/Dimitrijevic (4 *cr*; 26 *t*); Panda Photo/Pirovano (5 *t*; 26 *b*); Panda Photo/Sutter (53 *b*; 57 *t*); Panda Photo/Vigliotti (5 *b*; 24 *b*); Granata (4 *bl*; 5 *c*; 46; 53 *t*; 59 *bl*; 59 *br*); Granata/Archive (6; 7; 40; 41 *t*; 43 *t*; 43 *c*; 50; 51 *tl*; 51 *tr*; 63 *t*); Granata/ Francis(63 *b*); Granata/Briggs/Holland (4 *cl*).

DoGi s.r.l. has made every effort to identify the rights of third parties. We apologize in advance for any omissions or errors and will be very happy to insert timely corrections in subsequent editions of this work.